Dorothy Lynch Dressing

1 qt. jar

1 C. sugar
1/8 tsp. garlic salt
1 tsp. dry mustard
1 Tblsp. celery seed
1 tsp. salt
1 tsp. pepper
1 can tomato soup
1 C. salad oil
1/2 C vinegar

Put all ingredients in jar and shake well.

Better Homes and Gardens

SALAD BOOK

MEREDITH PRESS
New York Des Moines

Printed in the United States of America.
Ninth Printing, 1967.

FLAT FILLETS OF ANCHOVIE

You can serve sunshine—in salad

You're all set to scoop up fresh air and *sunshine*—the sunshine of spring vegetable gardens and autumn fruit-laden orchards. In a *salad*.

Here you capture the beauty, the vitality and goodness that's Nature, and you serve it *beautifully* to your family and your guests. It's theirs to feast the eye on, theirs to eat with a very special enjoyment. *And* theirs to achieve the pep and vigor that come with *good health*.

Turn pages and revel in sunshine. Here's inspiration to put new zest in marketing and in mealmaking. Here are the lush bowl salads with their bright, crisp vegetables, the homespun coleslaws and picnic potato salads, handsome fruit-salad luncheons, gay relish trays—all fun to fix and easy to serve. Salads that make a meal; salads that complement a meal.

Shall we start capturing salad sunshine!

Use fresh crisp greens, *peak-of-the-season vegetables, and full-flavored fruits to make salad that's a match for this. Off to a right start!*

Keep it simple, *casual—your salad will be as luscious, cool and inviting as this melon beauty (Honeydew Boat, page 27). You're unruffled, too!*

← ***Brimming with goodness,*** *this buffet bowl. Every bite's cool, delicious, and packed with vitamins.*

Help yourself to red-ripe tomato and spicy luncheon meat strips. For crunch, pick up green pepper, bias-cut Carrot Crisps, celery, radish. Now, top off with zippy extras—anchovies, olives, some Clear French Dressing (page 128).

This is just a sample of the wonderful salads you'll find in the pages ahead. Happy tossing to you!

A salad can be this handsome, luscious to eat

Pick the right dressing *to enhance the salad flavors. Pass it in attractive server, to spoon on; or present it as a dip for casual finger-salad nibbling.*

When dressing is for greens, add at the last minute so salad stays crisp.

Chill the plates *or bowls. Slide them in refrigerator till ready to use. Keeps salad fresh on trip to the table.*

Summer spectaculars—ice ring shown here (page 139 tells how); relishes and cocktail salads arranged atop crushed ice.

Be generous *when you slice or chunk salad ingredients. Generous slices, generous chunks.*

This makes your creation more beautiful, more interesting, reflects Nature's abundance. Here's what we mean—Avocado Sunburst (see page 21).

Serve salad with salad. *Here it's Chicken Salad in Raspberry Ring. Page 108 gives the recipe, the rest of the meal.*

For a buffet indoors or out, a salad bar is tempting summer fare. Set out a choice of vegetable or fruit salads and dressings, along with a platter of cold cuts, the bread basket, tall glasses of iced tea or coffee. Meal's made.

Begin with salad, *serve it as the main dish or the accompaniment, or let it be the lovely finish of a meal. Here potato salad's the main dish, relishes the accompaniment. For more serving ideas, see pages 145-149.*

Keep trims simple. *A pinwheel of three olive slices centered with red dot of pimiento gives party air to Chicken Buffet Molds (recipe page 110), yet it's quick, easy. For more garnish ideas and pictures, see pages 138-143.*

Look for this symbol. *Wherever you see it, you'll find a handy salad-making tip. How to seed grapes in a jiffy, best way to turn gelatin salad out of mold, other time-saving short cuts. See Tips listing in index.*

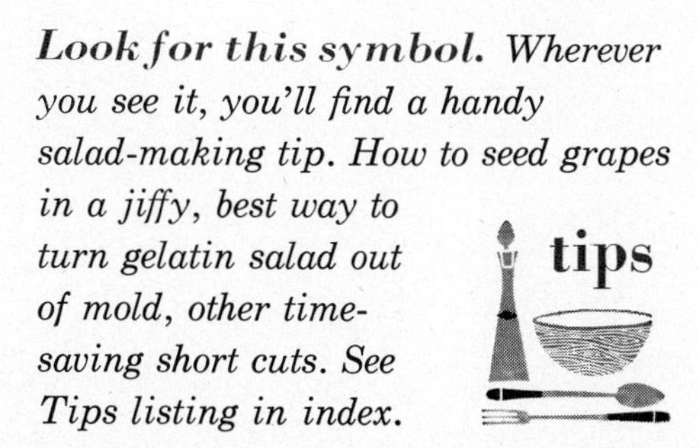

Summer masterpiece—lush fruit tray

Chilly chunks of lime sherbet, sprigs of mint accent fruit wreath of melon, bias-cut lemon-sprinkled banana, coconut-rolled pineapple rings, strawberry halves, and grapes

Contents

This seal tells you that every recipe in your Salad Book is *endorsed* by the Better Homes & Gardens Test Kitchen. Each food is tested over and over till it's rated as superior—in family appeal, practicality, and downright deliciousness.

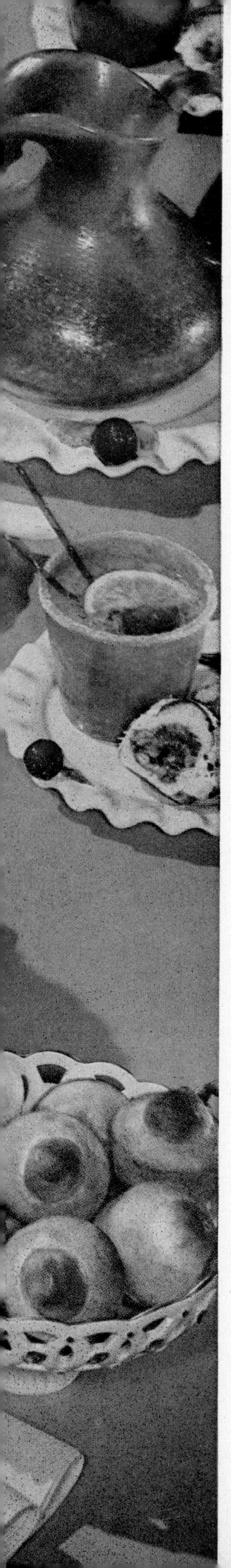

Fruit salads

Plentiful in quantity and priced for everyone are the fruits in today's markets. And is there one of the innumerable varieties you couldn't call beautiful? Whether served in an appetizer salad or in a salad accompaniment to a main dish, fruits are agreeable any time of the year.

Thrill to spring strawberries, to midsummer melons and peaches, to autumn apples with "snap" in both flavor and bite. Each season, in turn, offers its own dazzlers for *easy, luscious* fruit salads. But the "out-of-season" idea is gone for good, thanks to the wonders of canned and frozen and dried fruits. They are your year-round orchard and berry patch, your obliging, keep-on-call salad fruits.

Fruit is vitamin-filled, mineral-rich. There's a big *healthy* bonus of vitamin C in those orange slices and grapefruit sections, in that squirt of lemon or lime, in those giant red strawberries on the salad tray. Watching your waistline? Let simple fruit salads help you skimp on calories.

Here we bring you fruit plates and platters—these take you no time at all to arrange, lush and color-bright. And we bring chilly, sparkling gelatin molds and creamy frozen salads—these you fix ahead to await *your* convenience.

Tricks to bring out the best in fruit salads

Serve salad on *chilled* plates. Or for a glamor touch, bring salad to the table in a crushed-ice jacket (nestle bowl of salad in a larger bowl of crushed ice). Everything will look—and be—twice as cool, taste twice as good.

Dressings are important. Some are built in—as for Waldorf Salad, page 18, or Red-and-white-Fruit Mold, page 42. Exactly what kind of dressing to pass with tangy salads? With sweet salads? You'll find suggestions galore.

Even little things, like the way a pineapple is cut or a cantaloupe zigzagged in half, make a pretty difference. (Pictures show these tips, lots more.) Know how to choose a salad apple, to judge when pears are ripe, melons at flavor peak? We tell all.

Serve a fruit tower for a salad supper

← Let guests pick and choose. Bottom tier—slices of Frozen Fruit Medley, Frosted Grapes, red-plum halves, cantaloupe circles with cottage cheese and raspberries, honeydew cuts.

On center deck—bouquets of strawberries and Bibb lettuce, juicy pineapple slices. Up top—golden peach halves heaped with blueberries, accented with fragrant mint. Offer Poppy-seed Dressing. Pass hot rolls, pour icy limeade.

Drama for company—
fruit trays
that play up seasons

Fresh fruits—perfect for salad

August Afternoon Fruit Circle

Center large platter with bowlful of Cottage-cheese Delight, then circle it with fruits—scoops of watermelon, peach halves, slices of honeydew, halved strawberries and pineapple rings, big cantaloupe balls cut with a measuring tablespoon, and Banana Cuts.

Tuck a ruffle of lettuce around the edge and sprigs of fresh mint atop. Serve with thin slices of Butter-Pecan Bread, page 152, cups of hot coffee.

Cottage-cheese Delight:

2 cups drained large-curd cream-style cottage cheese
¼ cup pistachio nuts
½ cup halved seedless grapes
¼ cup mayonnaise
Salt

Lightly mix cheese, nuts, grapes, and mayonnaise. Add salt to taste. Garnish with cluster of grapes, if desired. Makes 4 servings.

Banana Cuts:

¼ cup honey
1½ teaspoons lemon or lime juice
3 all-yellow bananas
1 cup shredded coconut, toasted*

Combine honey and lemon juice. Peel bananas, and cut diagonally in thirds. Dip banana in honey mixture; then roll in coconut.

**To toast coconut*, spread shredded coconut in thin layer in shallow pan. Place in moderate oven (350°) and toast until delicately browned, 10 to 15 minutes. (Stir coconut or shake pan often, to toast evenly.)

Harvest Ring-around Platter

Stewed prunes, drained and pitted
Cream cheese, softened

• • •

All-yellow banana
Avocado, peeled and sliced thin
Unpared red apple, sliced thin
Lemon juice

• • •

Pineapple slices, drained and halved
Orange sections, drained
Tokay grapes

Stuff prunes with cream cheese. Peel banana, then run fork down it lengthwise all around for crinkly edge; slice diagonally. Sprinkle banana cuts, avocado, and apple with lemon juice to keep them bright.

Line platter with lettuce and arrange the fruits atop (some fruits are pretty lined up together in rows—like avocado slices alternated with half rings of pineapple, or apple slices alternated with orange sections).

Serve with Nippy Nectar Dressing, page 133. Nice for salad or evening snack (pass a tray of cheeses, some crisp crackers).

Pear Surprises

Dry drained, chilled canned pears well on paper towels. Fill hollow of each with cream cheese. Put a red cherry, pitted date, or fig (the surprise!) in center of two halves.

Seal the halves together with softened cream cheese. Using pastry tube, pipe cream-cheese ruffle along edges.

Use holly leaves for pear stems. Group on Parade-of-fruits Tray, as shown, or serve as individual salads on greens.

Summer Pineapple Platter—it's delicious

When fresh pineapple's at your market and watermelon's thumping-ripe, treat friends to this salad beauty.

Cut pineapple for dramatic serving, easy eating—see how on page 33. Between spokes of pineapple, heap perfect sections of grapefruit and orange, snowy cottage cheese. Center with crisp chunks from the luscious heart of the melon.

Parade-of-fruits Tray shows a gloriously tempting array you can feature even in snow time. What lovelier salad for your holiday buffet?

Choose a colorful variety of fruits. Here we show Pear Surprises (page 10), canned whole apricots and pineapple rings, stewed prunes, preserved kumquats, canned peach halves with cranberry-orange-relish filling, and Frosted Grapes (page 143). Crowning the platter are bright-red canned spiced crabapples.

Drain canned and stewed fruits and chill before arranging on greens.

A large platter or Lazy Susan, filled with this fruit beauty, can double as a centerpiece.

Perfect cool-off while you chat

It's Patio Plate, with a Tangy Tuna Mousse Square (page 113) in the center, potato chips and chilled fruits all around.

Honeydew ring has topknot of peach and plum halves, mint sprig. Pineapple ring, snipped and slipped through another, has stems-on maraschino cherries for trim. Frosted Grapes are sugar-sparkled (see how-to, page 143).

Serve with iced tea, sherbet, and dainty macaroons.

For the ladies—fruit plates

When you want to wow the girls, really set 'em talking, serve each a beautiful fruit plate—one of these tempting refreshers

Bridge Luncheon means a party!

Platemates here are a honeydew "boat" with cantaloupe balls, peach slices dipped in lemon juice, stems-on cherries, a smooth-skinned nectarine, purple plum, clusters of grapes.

Frosted Sandwich Square (page 157) with flower trim, is a four-decker make-ahead.

Nut Tree Fresh Fruit Plate

Papaya, sliced thin*
Red-skinned apple, sliced thin
Raw cranberries or pomegranate seeds**
Orange slices
Kumquats
Watermelon, cut in chunks
Fresh pineapple slices, cut in half
Whole tangerines, peeled
Pink grapefruit sections
Banana cuts
Whole fresh pears, pared
Small clusters of grapes
Cottage cheese or sherbet
Mint sprigs

Arrange chilled fruits around cottage cheese on individual plates, as shown. Tuck in mint. Serve with Waffled Orange Nut Bread, page 153.

***To prepare papayas:* Let them ripen at room temperature till skin turns yellow. Dunk in boiling water about 1 minute, then drop in cold water. Keep in refrigerator till time to use. Then, with knife, pull off skin, beginning at large end. Cut papayas in half, remove black seeds, slice, and serve.

*****To peel pomegranates:*** Break open under water so seeds won't spurt juice. The plump red seeds sink (have colander under water to catch them), dry membranes float.

For casual summer hospitality—refreshing Three-fruit Luncheon

On your prettiest plates, arrange chunks of watermelon, peach slices dipped in lemon juice, a bunch of grapes. Fill Deviled Eggs (page 118) using a pastry tube, and place on a ruffle of lettuce.

Sparkling ruby dressing in the tiny glass is made by combining 1 part lime juice, 2 parts honey, and enough paprika to color. Add simple trims—lime wedge perched on dressing glass, sprigs of mint.

Luscious—fruit "sampler"

At the Nut Tree in Vacaville, California, they heap each Fresh Fruit Plate with 9 to 13 fruits —this one boasts a dozen!

Center's cottage cheese or it could be sherbet. Pass Fluffy Fruit Dip (page 17), more toasty nut bread, and hot or iced coffee.

For a gray day, salad's a splash of color

For Tropicana Plate, alternate fresh or canned orange and grapefruit sections atop pineapple sticks. Split banana lengthwise and sprinkle with lemon juice. Add gay spiced crabapples. ←Serve with a cruet of Celery-seed Dressing, page 133.

Five-minute Pineapple Plate

Arrange lettuce on plates. On each, stack a pineapple ring, a slice of mild red or white onion (cut in quarters), and a slice of pickled beet. Top with parsley. Pass creamy French dressing. (Unusual, yes—good, too!)

Banana-Nut Salad

Split bananas in half lengthwise; dip in lemon juice. Arrange on greens. Blend about 1 tablespoon peanut butter with 1/4 cup mayonnaise and spread down centers of banana halves. Sprinkle with broken walnuts. If desired, trim with fan of orange sections.

When minutes fly, make jiffy fruit plates—

Pare, slice, stack—it's done

Sunny Winter Salad is for three. Each one helps himself to a half-slice of jellied cranberry sauce, a stack of pineapple and orange slices, and a mound of cottage cheese.

Sprightly green trim is sprigs of water cress.

Lunchtime? Let's have melon!

Fruit Festival is quick, cool, and refreshing. Fan out juicy slices of chilled honeydew and cantaloupe; grace them with clusters of plump green grapes and ripe red strawberry halves.

Lime wedge is to squeeze over melon. Like to serve a dressing, too? Honey Quickie, page 133, is just the thing for this lazy-day salad.

↓

↑

Create a rainbow of fruits

Plum Delicious, we call this one—on chilled plates, arrange ripe purple plums with golden pineapple rings, a handful of red raspberries, and an apricot half topped with coconut. Tuck in banana slices cut on the bias; sprinkle with lemon juice to keep them bright.

Trim with water cress. Serve with Celery-seed Dressing (page 133), dainty slices of nut bread, and tall, cool glasses of milk, to make it a luncheon.

for quickest, zip open cans

To brighten a blustery day—

How about serving Five-fruit Winter Treat? It's a colorful roundup of rich smooth avocado and plump green grapes, juicy orange sections, and red apple slices alternated with grapefruit.

Easy for the junior chef—

Children cooking? Speedy Cheese-Over-Pears is for them—fun to make *and* eat!

Drain chilled canned pear halves. Sandwich together with mayonnaise; place on greens. Top with shredded American cheese; trim with ripe olives.

Serve fresh-fruit appetizers for a party start

Light, tangy, and colorful—these fruit combinations are sure to whet appetites

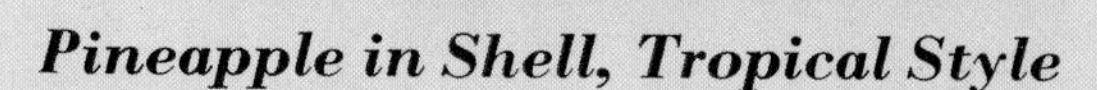

Pineapple in Shell, Tropical Style

Intriguing, simple—pass fresh pineapple appetizer in a natural "bowl," complete with leafy lid for trim. Surprise is shell full of half-slices, all ready to fork out. Each guest helps himself to several, then spoons marshmallow-y Fluffy Fruit Dip over the juicy pieces.

Pineapple Boats with Fruit

Cut pineapple, including leafy top, in half. Hollow out halves, leaving shells ½ inch thick. Cut out core; discard. Dice remaining pineapple. Refill shells with pineapple cubes, orange sections, and plump strawberries with caps left on. Chill. Just before serving, add plumes of mint. Insert cocktail picks at end of each shell. Arrange on tray—let guests help themselves.

Madrilene in Honeydew Cup

Chill cans of Madrilene consomme in refrigerator 3 hours (or 1 hour in freezer) to jelly. Cut small honeydew melons in half with zigzag line (see how, page 27). Remove seeds.

Spoon jellied consomme into center. Garnish with lime wedges. Serve with crackers.

← Appetizer, conversation-piece—it's Madrilene in Honedew Cup, perfect beginning for buffet luncheon on a lazy summer afternoon.

Pineapple in Shell, Tropical Style

Cut off top and bottom of a chilled, thoroughly ripe fresh pineapple. Then, with a sturdy sharp knife cut around fruit inside shell, first from top, then from the bottom, leaving a thin wall.

Remove the solid cylinder of pineapple. Cut it into fairly thin slices; then cut down through the stack to make half slices.

Pile up slices, then slide shell down over them. "Pin" bottom of pineapple back in place with toothpicks. Arrange filled shell and spiky top on tray.

Each guest helps himself to a slice or two and spoons Fluffy Fruit Dip over.

Fluffy Fruit Dip

1 cup sugar
⅔ cup light corn syrup
½ cup hot water
2 stiff-beaten egg whites
Dash salt
¼ teaspoon vanilla
¼ cup mayonnaise
1 tablespoon shredded orange peel

Combine sugar, corn syrup, and hot water. Heat slowly, stirring until sugar dissolves. Then boil without stirring to firm-ball stage (248°). Gradually beat hot syrup into stiff-beaten egg whites. Add salt and vanilla. Cool.

Fold in mayonnaise and orange peel. Serve as dressing for sliced pineapple or fruit salad, or as dunking dip for strawberries.

Frosty Fruit Cup

1 large bottle (about 2 cups) ginger ale
1 6-ounce can frozen tangerine-juice concentrate
1 12-ounce can frozen pineapple chunks
1 cup green seedless grapes
¼ cup maraschino cherry halves
2 cups cantaloupe balls
Mint sprigs

Combine the ginger ale and tangerine-juice concentrate; stir till concentrate dissolves. Pour into 2-quart refrigerator tray; freeze just to a mush (about 1 hour).

Thaw pineapple chunks just enough to eat (some ice crystals should remain); drain. Mix with grapes, cherries, and melon. Spoon ginger ale mixture into 8 sherbet glasses; top with fruits. Trim with mint.

Traditional Fruit Cup varies with the seasons. Here, a fall and winter combination — canned fruit cocktail is sparked with red apple wedges, orange sections, and avocado balls. Pastry partners are Cheese Straws.

In spring and summer, call on shiny strawberries, fresh pineapple and peaches, ripe golden melons. Try some in Frosty Fruit Cup.

Strawberries circling a bowlful of Fluffy Fruit Dip are a ready-ahead, easy-serve opener. Guests pick up by stems, and dip.

For *quick* dip, make *Marshmallow Dressing:* To ½ jar marshmallow creme, add 1 tablespoon *each* orange and lemon juice; whip very fluffy with electric or rotary beater. Fold in ¼ cup mayonnaise. Makes 1¼ cups.

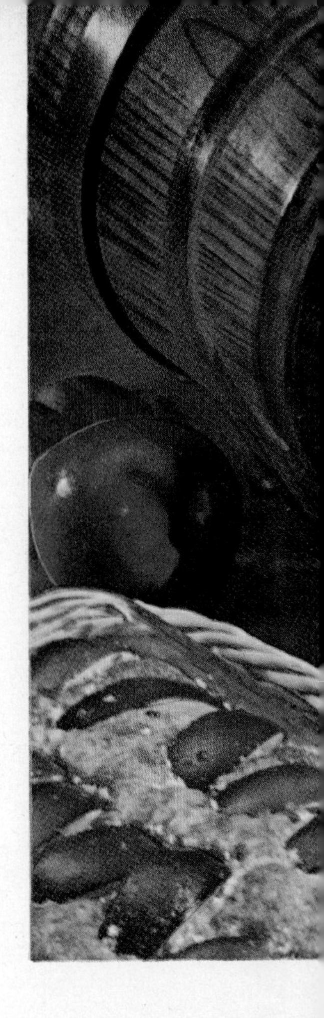

Star fruit dinner salads

like these crisp apple classics

Sparkling fresh-flavored fruit salads, teamed with pork roast, ham, and fried chicken, make homey meals that are hard to beat.

These fruit dinner salads—simple as grape-topped citrus sections; fancy as fruit-filled melons—are designed to go with the meat-and-vegetable course. But they can double as desserts, appetizers, main dishes—even look-at-*and*-eat centerpieces.

Apple beauties with the crispness of autumn are first on our dinner salad list. Here's classic Waldorf—five different ways; and apple with ham, apple with onion, apple with cinnamon candies. Use firm eating apples, tangy or mellow, and leave on the bright skins for color. Sprinkle lemon, lime, or pineapple juice over cut apples, to keep them light, or mix quickly with dressing.

Cooked Dressing is tops with apple, but for hurry-up salads, use mayonnaise-plus-milk, or a whipped cream dressing.

Basic Waldorf Salad

2 cups diced tart apples
1 tablespoon sugar
½ teaspoon lemon juice
Dash salt
1 cup 1-inch julienne celery sticks
½ cup broken California walnuts
¼ cup mayonnaise
½ cup whipping cream, whipped

Sprinkle apple cubes with sugar, lemon juice, and salt. Add celery and nuts.

Fold mayonnaise into whipped cream. Gently fold into apple mixture. Chill. Serve in lettuce-lined bowl. Makes 6 servings.

Date-Marshmallow Waldorf: Reduce celery to ½ cup and add ½ cup cut-up pitted dates and 4 marshmallows, quartered.

← Curl of red apple skin cups around this crunchy apple salad, to lend a party air. Recipe for Waldorf Spiral Salad tells how to make it.

Shiny scarlet eating apples, firm and tangy, spill from the wooden bucket. They're perfect for salads — some have already been cut into crisp juicy wedges for this hearty Apple-ball and Ham Salad (page 20).

Red Grape Waldorf: Add 1 cup halved and seeded Emperor grapes to basic recipe. (See how to seed grapes below.)

Orange Waldorf: Reduce celery to ½ cup and add ½ cup orange slices or Mandarin orange sections.

Snip! Seed grapes in a jiffy—

Use kitchen scissors to cut grapes in half; remove seeds with another snip or two. Grapes are ready to use in salad.

Waldorf Spiral Salad

- 6 red apples
- 4 cups cold water
- ⅓ cup lemon juice, fresh, frozen, or canned
- 1 cup diced celery
- ⅓ cup seedless raisins, plumped
- 1 cup tiny marshmallows
- ¼ cup mayonnaise
- ¼ cup heavy cream, whipped
- ½ cup coarsely broken California walnuts
- 6 lettuce cups

Pare apples very thick, being sure each paring is long and unbroken. Measure water and add *3 tablespoons* of lemon juice; drop parings in to keep color bright.

Core pared apples and dice fine; sprinkle with remaining lemon juice. Combine apple cubes, celery, raisins, marshmallows, and mayonnaise. Fold in whipped cream. Just before serving, add nuts.

Curl each paring into cup shape on lettuce. Fill with salad. Makes 6 servings.

Know your salad apples

Crisp red-cheeked ***Delicious,*** with five rounded points on the blossom end, is mellow, sweet, and juicy; with a fruity fragrance.

Golden Delicious has a speckled bright-yellow skin, a brisk flavor. *And* it doesn't darken when cut, making it ideal for salads.

Crispy yellow ***Grimes Golden*** is noted for its distinctive tart flavor.

Rosy-cheeked ***Jonathans, McIntosh,*** and ***Staymans*** are juicy, tart, and crunchy. McIntosh and Stayman are at their best in fall and early winter.

Winesap is a winter-spring apple with glossy red skin, tart winelike flavor. It "pops" with juice.

Yellow Newtown has pale yellow-green skin, is juicy, fresh-flavored, firm, long-keeping.

Apple-ball and Ham Salad

- 8 pared tart apples
- 2 tablespoons lemon juice, fresh, frozen, or canned
- 2 cups cubed cooked ham
- 1 cup diced celery
- ½ cup mayonnaise or salad dressing
- ¼ cup light cream or top milk
- ½ cup (2 ounces) crumbled blue cheese

Make balls from the apples, using melon-ball cutter or measuring teaspoon. Sprinkle balls with lemon juice. Combine with ham and celery.

Blend mayonnaise and cream. Add to apple mixture and toss. Sprinkle with blue cheese. Trim with a star of red-skinned apple wedges, fluff of parsley. Makes 8 to 10 servings.

Apple-stick Relish

- 3 unpared tart apples
- ⅔ cup chopped onion
- ½ cup chopped dill pickle
- ½ cup sugar
- ¼ cup vinegar

Core apples and cut in *small* strips. Mix with onion and pickle. Combine sugar and vinegar; toss with apple mixture. Chill. Serve as meat accompaniment. Makes 6 servings.

For salads, use tiny marshmallows, or cut up big ones: dip kitchen scissors in confectioners' sugar first—no sticking.

Cinnamon-apple Salad

- 6 tart apples
- ¾ cup red cinnamon candies
- 2 cups water
- 1 3-ounce package cream cheese
- 2 tablespoons milk
- 1 teaspoon lemon juice
- ⅓ cup pitted dates, cut up
- 1 9-ounce can (1 cup) pineapple tidbits, drained
- 2 tablespoons chopped walnuts
- Salad greens

Pare and core apples. Cook candies in water till dissolved. Add apples and cook slowly, uncovered, till just tender, about 15 to 20 minutes. Turn once during cooking. Chill in syrup several hours; turn once while chilling.

Blend cream cheese, milk, and lemon juice. Add dates, pineapple, and nuts.

Drain apples and place atop salad greens. Stuff centers with cream-cheese mixture. Makes 6 servings.

Apple Dessert Salad

- 2 unpared apples, cored and sliced
- Lemon juice
- Lettuce, or green apple leaves
- 1 3-ounce package cream cheese
- 2 tablespoons finely diced candied ginger

Sprinkle apple slices with lemon juice to keep them bright, if necessary. Arrange apple slices in fan shape atop lettuce on dessert plates.

Whip softened cream cheese; blend in ginger to taste. Add a dash of salt, if desired. Heap mound of this mixture on lettuce beside apple fans. Serve with crisp crackers. Makes 2 to 3 servings.

Avocado Sunburst is refreshing as early spring—slices of avocado tucked between orange sections, topped with sprinkling of strawberry halves. Final touch: a flag of water cress.

For special meals, serve salads with an avocado accent

Rich buttery avocados team up elegantly with tart orange and grapefruit sections, crisp apple wedges, ripe tomato slices.

Ripen avocados at room temperature. Test by pressing avocado gently between *palms* of hands. It's ripe if it yields readily.

Store ripe avocados in refrigerator's vegetable crisper. To store part of one, brush cut edges with lemon juice; wrap closely in saran wrapping or aluminum foil. Refrigerate.

Avocado-Tomato Plate

Cut peeled ripe avocado half in strips; fan out over tomato slices arranged on lettuce. Garnish with lemon wedge.

Avocado Fruit Toss

1 small head lettuce
½ head curly endive
2 medium, ripe avocados
1 cup orange sections
1 cup grapefruit sections
Clear French dressing
Pomegranate seeds, if desired

Tear lettuce and endive into bite-size pieces. Halve and seed avocados. Peel; slice into bowl. Add orange and grapefruit sections. Toss with enough clear French dressing to coat. Sprinkle with pomegranate seeds. Makes 8 to 9 servings.

Halve and seed avocados; slice, dice, or serve as half shells

Cut fruit in half lengthwise; then cup it between palms of hands and gently twist halves apart.

Tap seed with sharp edge of knife. Lift or pry seed gently out.

Here, avocado halves filled with Lobster Salad (page 104) are high point of fruit platter. Serve tangy fruit relishes on half shell, too.

Spark winter meals with sunny citrus salads

Pink-grapefruit Refresher

4 pink grapefruit, pared and sectioned (see how, opposite page)
Lettuce or romaine
1½ cups fresh cranberries, halved*
3 to 4 tablespoons sugar*
Parsley or water cress

Drain grapefruit sections and pile atop bed of lettuce or romaine. Sweeten cranberries with sugar; mound them in center of grapefruit sections. Garnish with parsley or water cress. Makes 8 servings. Pass Honey Dressing, page 132.

*Or use 1 cup pomegranate seeds, and omit sugar.

Orange Stuffed-Prune Stackup

Orange slices
Salad greens
Prunes, softened and pitted
Cottage cheese
Walnut halves

Place orange slices on salad greens. Stuff prunes with cottage cheese and top with walnut halves. Arrange on orange slices. Plan three stackups for each serving.

Fruit-filled Orange

Slice tops from large oranges. With grapefruit knife or paring knife, remove orange sections. Combine orange sections with banana and plum slices; other fruits in season. Refill orange shells with fruit mixture. Trim with mint. Pass Honeyberry Dressing.

Honeyberry Dressing: Beat smooth ½ cup jellied cranberry sauce. Stir in ¼ cup honey and 1 teaspoon lemon juice. Makes ¾ cup.

Halloween Party Salads: Cut tiny jack-o-lantern faces in the orange shells before filling with salad. Add clove stems to tops, and place on filled shells for "lids."

Ambrosia Salad

¾ cup diced orange
2 flecked-with-brown bananas, sliced
½ cup seedless grapes
¼ cup pitted dates, cut up
3 tablespoons lemon juice
¼ cup flaked coconut

Combine fruits; sprinkle with lemon juice; chill. Fold in Creamy Mayonnaise or fluffy Cooked Dressing. Serve on crisp lettuce. Sprinkle on coconut. Makes 4 to 6 servings.

Luncheon specialty: Heap salad in Party Grapefruit Baskets

Halve grapefruit. Cut around each section; remove all, leaving membrane intact. Then snip out whole membrane with scissors.

For the handles: Leaving 1 inch uncut in center of opposite sides, cut around each grapefruit half, ⅓ inch below the rim.

To shape basket handles, lift up the two resulting cut strips and tie their centers together with bow of white or colored ribbon.

Mix grapefruit and orange sections in these inviting ways

Citrus Circle features "grapefruit-orange" atop half-rings of pineapple, greens. Trim: more fruit sections, ripe olives.

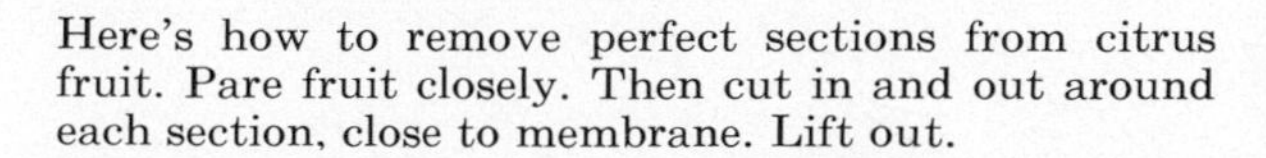

January Fruit Bowl holds an overlapping circle of juicy grapefruit sections and orange slices. Avocado cut with melon-ball cutter makes the topper. Curly endive is tucked in for trim.

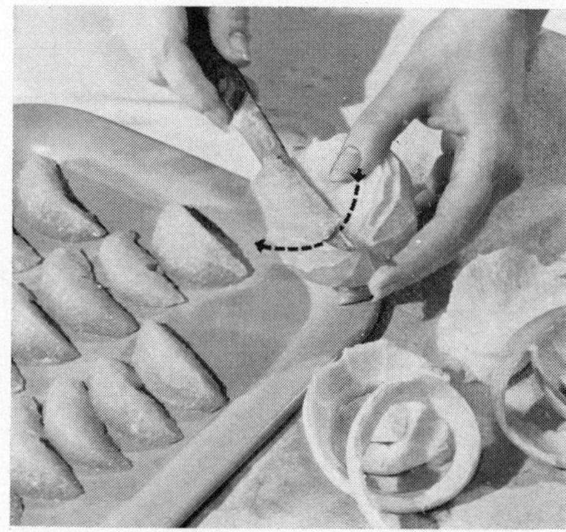

Here's how to remove perfect sections from citrus fruit. Pare fruit closely. Then cut in and out around each section, close to membrane. Lift out.

Fruit-filled Orange

Jaunty fruit cup, trimmed with mint and served with Honeyberry Dressing, is perfect choice for appetizer, dinner salad, light dessert.

Fill baskets with fruit salad containing the grapefruit sections. Top with scoops of sherbet.

Make midsummer magic with rainbow of melons: Presto—perfect salad!

No magician's cloak needed, either, to produce a melon salad masterpiece.

Start with a wedge, slice, or zigzagged half of melon. Add scoops of tart sherbet, slices of spicy ham, or bouquets of fresh fruits. A pert flag of mint, parsley, or water cress completes the magic.

Vary these refreshers by trying all the melons. Cantaloupe, honeydew, and watermelon are old favorites. Also delightful in salads are honeyballs, Persians, casabas, and cranshaws.

Honeyball is part honeydew, part cantaloupe. It's a small melon, very sweet and juicy; green inside, creamy white outside.

Look-alike cousin to cantaloupe, Persian melon is green under its netting, even when ripe. It's fragrant, mildly sweet.

The casaba resembles a squash, with its wrinkled buttery-yellow skin, but underneath it's soft, creamy white, juicy. Casabas are tops in October and November.

For mixed-fruit salads, try the delicate cranshaw melon, a casaba-Persian melon cross. Under the gold-splashed green skin, it's juicy, almost spice-flavored.

Identify melons with key below

Melons pictured at left include (1) casaba; (2) refrigerator-size watermelon; (3) Persian; (4) cranshaw; (5) honeyball; (6) cantaloupe; and (7) honeydew. (Recipes on pages 26, 27.)

Play up melon beauty, in a salad centerpiece

Perfect porch supper plan: glamorous Melon "Basket" salad, thin ham slices, hot rolls, and dessert.

Melon "Basket"

Pare whole honeydew melon. Mark it in tenths or twelfths with toothpicks; then, leaving about a 2-inch circle uncut at top and bottom, with sharp knife remove every other wedge.

Discard seeds and stringy portion. Cut thin slice from one end of melon and stand "basket" in center of platter. Arrange cut-out wedges spoke fashion on the platter, placing them at the openings in the melon.

Fill center of basket with raspberries or other berries. Top with tiny grape leaves.

Arrange small bunches of grapes, plums, and lemon wedges around melon. Offer a choice of fruit dressings.

Persian Platter

Halve Persian melon and remove seeds. Cut into chunks, pare, and arrange on a platter. Place cups of Bibb lettuce at ends of platter; fill with fresh ripe strawberries.

Melon Wedge-Pineapple Bowl

Cut miniature watermelon and large honeydew melon into lengthwise slices. Cut leafy top from fresh pineapple; then cut pineapple into long wedges and remove core. Cut into pineapple so it's easy to eat (see page 33).

Arrange fruit slices in large bowl, with leafy pineapple top, clusters of grapes. Use as centerpiece; serve later as salad.

Honeydew-Ham Starter

Sandwich *paper-thin* slices of Prosciutto (Italian-style ham) between juicy crescents of honeydew melon. Add parsley fluff. Serve as an appetizer for supper or brunch.

Honeydew Boat

Top a honeydew wedge with trio of tart lime wedges and tiny bunch of green seedless grapes. Garnish with mint sprig. Serve as appetizer or light dessert.

Honeyball a la Mode

Halve whole honeyball melon and remove seeds. Cut into plump round slices; pare. Top each with scoops of raspberry sherbet. For accent: perky mint. Serve as accompaniment to fried chicken, or as dessert salad.

When is a melon ripe?

Experts admit it's hard to tell, and signs of ripeness vary with the different melons.

Watermelon and cantaloupe must ripen on the vine to be sweet and flavorful. Spot a ready cantaloupe by the smooth indented "button" on its stem end, where the melon parted easily from the stem. Look, too, for coarse corky netting over green-tinged light yellow skin.

Watermelon is harder to judge. Best signs to look for are good figure, fresh green or gray skin with yellow underside, and velvety bloom. Best of all, buy a cut melon or ask the dealer to plug a whole one for you to sample. The time-honored "thumping test" may mislead. Ripe juicy melon gives a dull muffled sound when slapped with the palm —but so does a dry one!

Check color on the other melons. Look for creamy-yellow honeydews and honeyballs, butter-yellow casabas, cranshaws that are light green dappled with gold. Only Persians remain quite green, under their netting. All these melons will ripen at room temperature.

Perfect honeydew and honeyball, casaba, Persian, and cranshaw melons yield to gentle pressure on the blossom end—but so will unripe ones, if anyone has punched them first.

The sniff test is a final guide. Except for watermelon and casaba, melons have a wonderful fruity fragrance when ready to eat.

To zigzag edges of melon bowls:

Thrust knife into center at angle; pull out. Make next cut at opposite angle. Repeat around melon.

For Melon, Buffet-style—heap varicolored balls in scalloped shell

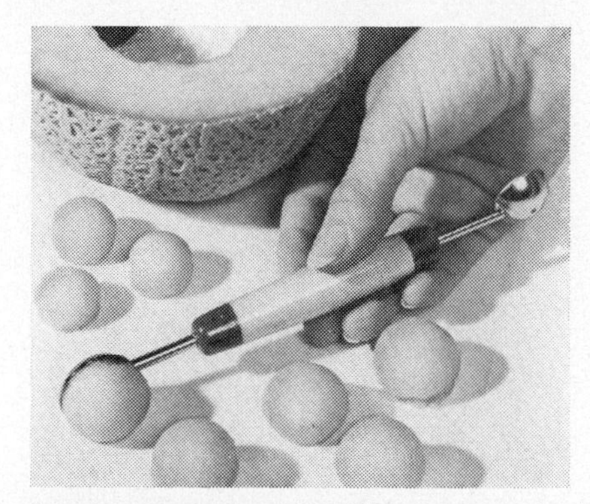

Cut watermelon, honeydew, and cantaloupe balls with melon-ball cutter or measuring teaspoon. Make scalloped shell from watermelon half, after removing balls. Mark and cut scallops, using saucer edge as guide. Fill shell.

Whole lunch for hot summer day—Fruited Honeydew served with cottage cheese and strawberries, nut-bread sandwiches, iced tea. Pare honeydew circles; top with cuts of peach, banana, plum, and apricot. Trim with cherries, sprigs of mint.

For quick-fix salad—ice a melon, spice peaches

Spiced Peaches, all ready to serve in lettuce cups, are make-aheads that can be fixed in a jiffy.

Combine 1 No. 2½ can peach halves, 1 tablespoon vinegar, 1 to 2 sticks cinnamon, 1 teaspoon cloves.

Heat to boiling; then simmer 5 minutes. Chill. Drain, stud with cloves.

Honeyball with Fruit Topper

Lettuce
Thin slices honeyball or honeydew melon
Lemon juice
Fresh sweet cherries, pitted
Grapes, halved and seeded
Chopped pecans

Arrange lettuce on salad plates. Top with slices of melon; sprinkle with lemon juice. Spill cherries, grapes, and chopped pecans over melon. Pass a fruit dressing.

Melonette Mix

Toss together chilled melon balls—cantaloupe, honeydew, and watermelon. Heap in lettuce-lined salad bowls. Sprinkle handful of fresh raspberries over each serving.

Garnish with fluff of parsley and row of bias-cut banana slices at side. Pass a bowl of Celery-seed Dressing.

Chilly treat for the middle of July is this luscious Melon-Berry Bowl a la Iceberg.
Line bowl with juicy wedges of cantaloupe. Heap center with plump whole strawberries, or blueberries.
Garnish with mint; circle with ice cubes.

Apple-Melon Toss with Cheese

2 cups diced unpared apple
1 cup celery slices
1½ cups cantaloupe or honeydew balls

• • •

½ cup dairy sour cream
⅓ cup mayonnaise
2 ounces blue cheese, crumbled
(⅓ to ½ cup)

Mix apple cubes, celery slices, and melon balls. Blend sour cream and mayonnaise; stir in blue cheese. Add to apple mixture and toss lightly. Chill. Serve in lettuce cups. Makes 4 to 5 servings.

Carnival Cantaloupe Rings

1 cup diced fresh pineapple
2 cups strawberries
1 cup honeydew melon balls
6 pared cantaloupe rings, 1 inch thick
Shredded lettuce

Mix pineapple, strawberries, and melon balls. Place cantaloupe rings on lettuce and fill centers with fruit mixture. Pass fruit dressing, if desired. Makes 6 servings.

Peach Salad Suggestions

Golden Peach Plate: Crown canned peach half with cottage cheese; top with chopped walnuts or bits of candied ginger. Trim plate with curly endive, red apple slices, cherries.

Peach-Pineapple Towers: Circle platter with chilled drained pineapple rings, centered with peach halves. Top with whipped cream flavored with mint jelly. Finish with apricot halves and sprinkle of strawberries.

Be gentle with strawberries, store with hulls

To be sure strawberries will be at the peak of their juicy goodness when served, take good care of them.

Sort berries, but don't wash or hull. Spread them out on a tray or cooky sheet to prevent mashing; refrigerate.

Just before serving, wash the berries, leaving hulls on, so neither juice nor flavor is lost. *Now* hull, if desired.

Enjoy the delicate flavor of juicy pear salads

For luncheon—Pink Pears

Inside rosy pear halves, there's a nippy surprise of cream cheese mixed with bits of candied ginger.

Mint candy leaves, cinnamon-stick stem, and cream-cheese frill deck the outside. Blush is brushed on.

Serve on lettuce, or group several in one section of a fruit platter.

Pear-Waldorf with Swiss Cheese

1 cup diced, pared fresh pears
3 tart medium apples, pared and diced (about 3 cups)
2 tablespoons lemon juice, fresh, frozen, or canned

• • •

¾ cup diced Swiss cheese
½ cup celery slices
½ cup broken California walnuts
⅔ cup mayonnaise or salad dressing

• • •

Salad greens

Sprinkle pear and apple cubes with lemon juice. Add cheese, celery, and nuts. Toss lightly with mayonnaise. Chill. Serve on salad greens. Trim with pear wedges or apple rings, if desired. Makes 6 servings.

Or, heap salad mixture on greens in center of large plate and trim with Pear Crown: Arrange 6 or 8 pared fresh, or canned, pear halves, pointed ends up, around salad, to form crown. Top each pear half with a maraschino cherry (with stem on).

Cheesy Sliced Pears

Chill ripe pears. Core; then cut each one in four crosswise slices. Spread cut surfaces generously with sharp spreading cheese. Reassemble each pear. Top with fluff of parsley, if desired. Serve on crisp salad greens.

Pink Pears

Chill canned pear halves and drain; dry well on paper towels. To tint, add a few drops of water to red food coloring; daub on pears with bit of paper towel or paper napkin to give pink blush.

Fill hollows with softened cream cheese mixed with a little finely chopped candied ginger. Seal two pear halves together with cream cheese; pipe on cream-cheese ruffle.

Put small pieces of stick cinnamon on top for stems. Cut leaf-shaped candy mints in half for leaves. Or, roll out green gumdrops on sugar between waxed paper; with scissors or knife cut out leaves.

Serve pears on crisp lettuce.

For salad, pick a ripe pear

Pears taste best if picked before they're ready to eat, then ripened indoors, to mellow juicy goodness. Some pears are ripened before they are sold, some aren't. Home-ripen pears at room temperature, in the sack or box in which they were purchased.

Bartletts will turn from green to deep red or golden yellow, depending on the variety.

Comice and *Anjou* pears may be green-skinned even when ripe, but they'll yield to gentle thumb-and-finger pressure. Ripe *Boscs* wear cinnamon-brown jackets flecked with gold. Hold ripened pears in refrigerator.

Halve chilled pears, core, garnish—these salads are table-ready!

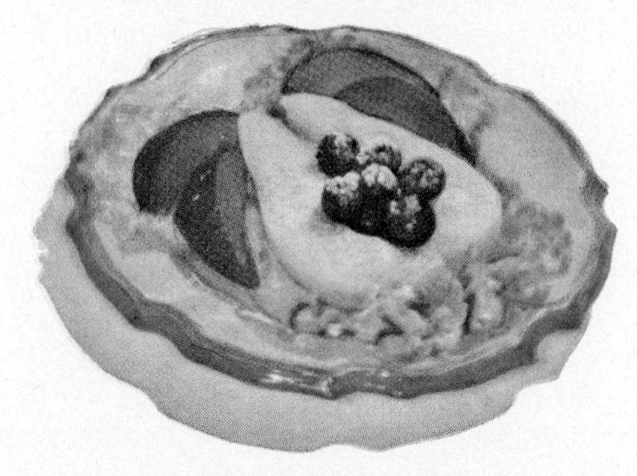

4th of July Pear holds blueberries with a sprinkle of confectioners' sugar. "Wings" are ripe plum slices, trim—lettuce ruffle.

Grape leaves accent Pear Salad Dessert, simplicity itself—chunk of cream cheese and cluster of grapes with chilled pear half.

Perfect choice for salad use—pears ripe for eating, plump and juicy

Bell-shaped Bartletts arrive in late summer, some dressed in scarlet, some in gold. Underneath, they're juicy, mellow-sweet.

Fragrant buttery Comice pears have a reputation for fine quality, size, and beauty. They're often packed in holiday gift boxes.

Green-skinned Anjous are really ripe, full of spicy flavor, and bursting with juice. Buy them in winter and early spring.

Sugar-sweet Bosc pears (also called Fall Russets) are firm under their cinnamon-brown skins. They're tops in midwinter.

For a tropical touch —pineapple salads

Golden chunks of pineapple, juicy crisp and delicately sweet, add a spot of sunshine to fruit and vegetable salads.

For quick use, buy canned or frozen pineapple. When there's time for elegance, try your hand with a whole fresh pineapple—use even the shell to make an intriguing all-in-one salad bowl and centerpiece.

Be sure fresh pineapple is ripe. Test by snapping the side of the fruit with thumb and finger. Hollow thud means try another one; dull sound says it's ready.

Store uncut pineapple in a cool place away from sunlight (but *not* in the refrigerator). After pineapple is cut, wrap unused pieces in aluminum foil or saran wrapping; store them in the refrigerator up to 3 or 4 days.

Pineapple-Cheese Cart Wheel

1 3-ounce package cream cheese
2 tablespoons chopped mixed candied fruits and peels
8 pineapple slices (1 No. 2½ can), chilled and drained
Curly endive
Cooked pitted prunes, chilled

Whip softened cream cheese to spreading consistency. (If necessary, blend in 1 to 2 teaspoons light cream or pineapple syrup.) Stir in candied fruits and peels.

Spread cheese mixture on 4 pineapple slices; top with remaining slices. Cut each "sandwich" in half. For each serving, turn two halves on edge, on curly endive.

Trim edges of cream cheese (peeking between pineapple slices) with more candied fruits and peels if desired. Garnish each plate with several prunes. Makes 4 servings.

Pineapple-Nut Sandwich: Substitute ¼ cup chopped walnuts for candied fruit. Place whole "sandwiches" on endive.

Sprinkle handful of halved ripe strawberries over each. Omit the prunes.

For summer evening supper: Frosty Pineapple Pastel

Hollow out half a pineapple. Core and dice fruit; heap back in shell. Top with rainbow of sherbets. Circle with crushed ice and fresh fruits.

Cut ripe pineapple into easy-to-eat pieces; then serve in shell or out

First remove stem from pineapple. Hold the fruit in one hand and with the other twist the prickly top firmly, until it comes off of pineapple.

If necessary, protect hands with cloth or gloves.

With a sturdy sharp knife cut pineapple into ½-inch slices. Then trim off the outside edges, being sure to remove all the eyes. Core each slice with center of doughnut cutter, or cooky cutter.

If desired, cut rings in cubes. Mix with fresh strawberries for special treat.

Want to serve pineapple with its natural trim? Chill, then cut in quarters. Cut the hard core from each section, then loosen fruit from skin, close to eyes.

Cut loosened part crosswise in 3 or 4 sections. If desired, cut in bite-size pieces. Serve in jacket (see page 11).

Fluffy Pineapple-Cheese Salad

1 No. 2 can (2½ cups) pineapple chunks
2 cups cream-style cottage cheese
2 cups tiny marshmallows
1 tablespoon lemon juice
½ cup pitted dates, cut up
Lettuce
Whole pitted dates

Drain pineapple, reserving ¼ cup syrup. Combine reserved syrup, cottage cheese, marshmallows, lemon juice, and cut-up dates. Serve on crisp lettuce and frame with pineapple chunks. Top each serving with whole pitted dates. Makes 6 servings.

Another time, center a fresh-fruit tray with this salad mixture. Omit the whole dates and sprinkle the pineapple chunks over.

Pineapple-Carrot Toss

1 No. 2 can (2½ cups) pineapple tidbits
2 cups shredded carrots
⅔ cup seedless raisins, plumped
Mayonnaise to moisten
Salad greens

Drain pineapple, reserving syrup. Combine pineapple, carrot, and raisins. Chill. Add a little pineapple syrup to mayonnaise; add to carrot mixture; toss. Serve on crisp salad greens. Makes 6 servings.

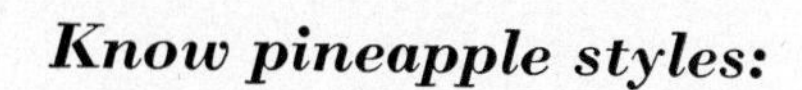

Know pineapple styles:

Crushed pineapple—is just right to use in molded salads, salad dressings

Tidbits—more dainty than chunks. Use in tossed salad, fruit cup

Chunks—canned *and* frozen cubes for all-purpose use

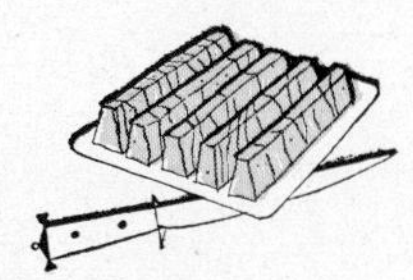

Spears—juicy fingers to fan out on salad plates, trays

Slices—to put in, under, or atop salads

Company? Make frozen salad ahead

Frosty Fruit Squares

2 tablespoons sugar
1 tablespoon enriched flour
½ cup honey
⅓ cup lemon juice
1 beaten egg
1 1-pound can fruit cocktail, drained
1 cup ripe banana slices
⅓ cup diced orange sections
¼ cup halved maraschino cherries
1 cup heavy cream, whipped

In saucepan, combine sugar, flour, and honey; bring to boiling. Cook 1 minute, stirring constantly. Gradually stir lemon juice into egg, then blend in small amount of honey mixture. Return to remaining hot mixture.

Bring just to boiling, stirring constantly. Remove from heat. Cool. Stir in fruits; fold in whipped cream. Pour into refrigerator tray. Freeze firm. Cut in serving-size pieces. Trim as shown below. Makes 6 servings.

Marshmallowy Squares: Omit fruit cocktail, banana, and orange. Add 1 No. 2 can pineapple tidbits, drained, 1 cup drained canned seedless grapes, and 3 cups tiny marshmallows. Freeze in two 1-quart trays. Makes 10 to 12 servings.

Frozen Fruit Medley

1 No. 2½ can (3½ cups) fruit cocktail
1 package lemon-flavored gelatin
1 cup boiling water
2 tablespoons lemon juice, fresh, frozen, or canned
2 3-ounce packages cream cheese
½ cup mayonnaise or salad dressing
1½ cups tiny marshmallows
¼ cup drained quartered maraschino cherries
1 cup heavy cream, whipped

Drain fruit cocktail, reserving 1 cup syrup. Dissolve gelatin in water; add reserved syrup and lemon juice. Chill till partially set.

Soften cream cheese, add mayonnaise and beat till smooth. Add to gelatin mixture, mixing well. Stir in fruit cocktail, marshmallows, and cherries. Fold in whipped cream.

To match picture on page 8, make a salad mold from the fruit-cocktail can. Remove both ends; flatten can slightly to an oval shape. Place heavy-duty aluminum foil over one end. Pour half of mixture into can, remainder into refrigerator tray. (Or pour it into two cans, if you have them.)

Freeze several hours or overnight. Slice and place atop lettuce. Makes 12 servings.

No need to bother with dessert when these luscious Rosy Fruit-cocktail Slices come to table. Serve the rich fruity salad with mayonnaise and Celery-seed Dressing. Top with cherries.

Rosy Fruit-cocktail Slices

2 3-ounce packages cream cheese
1 cup mayonnaise
1 cup heavy cream, whipped
1 No. 2½ can (3½ cups) fruit cocktail, well drained
½ cup drained maraschino cherries, quartered
2½ cups (about 24) large marshmallows, cut up, or tiny marshmallows
Few drops red food coloring or maraschino-cherry juice

Soften cream cheese; blend with mayonnaise. Fold in remaining ingredients.

Pour salad mixture into two 1-quart round ice-cream or freezer containers, or other containers shown at right. Freeze firm, about 6 hours or overnight. To serve, let stand out a few minutes, then remove from container, slice, and place on crisp lettuce. Trim with cherries (stems on), small lettuce leaves.

Makes 10 to 12 servings.

←

Fruit trim makes salad special

Trio of orange sections and bright red cherry give color touch to party salad. Each Frosty Fruit Square is rich with whipped cream, thick with orange sections and cherries, banana rounds, fruit cocktail.

Mold salads all shapes in trays, cans

Quickest way to freeze salad mixture is in a refrigerator tray.

Chill salad till firm; cut in slices, squares, or wedges. Make wedges by cutting trayful of salad in 3 equal pieces, then cutting each piece into two fat triangles.

For round slices, mold salad in No. 2 or 2½ cans or in paper ice-cream or freezer cartons.

For oval slices, follow directions given in the recipe for Frozen Fruit Medley, opposite page.

Fill containers with salad and freeze firm.

Allow salad to stand out several minutes before removing. Then:

Cut around bottom of round can with can opener. Push salad out with end of can. Slice.

Push salad out of oval mold with spatula.

Split paper containers; peel from salad.

Strawberry-Pineapple Cups

1 9-ounce can (1 cup) pineapple tidbits
1 cup sliced drained strawberries, sweetened fresh, or thawed frozen
1 cup tiny marshmallows
¼ cup broken pecans
1 envelope (1 tablespoon) unflavored gelatin
¼ cup mayonnaise or salad dressing
1 cup heavy cream, whipped

Drain pineapple, reserving syrup. Combine pineapple and strawberries, marshmallows, and nuts. Soften gelatin in 3 tablespoons of the reserved pineapple syrup. Heat remaining syrup just to boiling and add to gelatin. Stir to dissolve. Add to fruit mixture.

Fold mayonnaise into whipped cream, then fold into fruit-nut mixture. Fill paper bake cups placed in muffin pans. Freeze firm. Makes 16 servings.

Strawberry-Pineapple Cups do double duty. Here they are in-the-cup dessert salads. For dinner, remove cups, serve on greens.

These salads chill overnight for perfect flavor

Cranberry-Tokay Salad

2 cups fresh cranberries
1 cup sugar
1 cup Tokay grapes
¼ cup broken California walnuts
½ cup heavy cream, whipped

Put cranberries through food chopper, using coarse blade. Stir in sugar. Let drain overnight; stir, pressing lightly to remove excess juice. (Use juice in fruit punch.)

Cut grapes in half and remove seeds. Add grapes and nuts to well-drained cranberry mixture. Just before serving, fold in whipped cream. Mound in lettuce cups. Garnish with clusters of grapes. Serve immediately. Makes 4 to 5 servings.

Twenty-four Hour Salad

3 beaten egg yolks
2 tablespoons sugar
2 tablespoons vinegar
2 tablespoons pineapple syrup
1 tablespoon butter or margarine
Dash salt

• • •

2 cups drained canned pitted white cherries
2 cups drained canned pineapple tidbits
2 pared oranges, cut in pieces, drained
2 cups tiny marshmallows or 16 large marshmallows, cut in eighths
1 cup heavy cream, whipped

Combine egg yolks, sugar, vinegar, pineapple syrup, butter, and salt in top of double boiler. Cook over *hot, not boiling*, water, till thick, stirring constantly. Cool.

Stir in cherries, pineapple tidbits, orange pieces, and marshmallows. Fold in whipped cream. Spoon gently into serving bowl. Chill 24 hours in refrigerator, so flavors blend to mellow fruity perfection.

To match picture, trim salad with orange sections, maraschino cherries, and green seedless grapes. Tuck in sprigs of mint. Serve as a dinner salad or dessert, or let it double for both. Makes 6 to 8 servings.

Apple Snow Salad

1 9-ounce can (1 cup) crushed pineapple
2 beaten eggs
½ cup sugar
Dash salt
3 tablespoons lemon juice, fresh, frozen, or canned
2 cups finely diced unpared apple
½ cup finely diced celery
1 cup heavy cream, whipped

Drain pineapple, reserving syrup. Add water to pineapple syrup to make ½ cup. Combine eggs, sugar, salt, lemon juice, and syrup mixture. Cook over low heat, stirring constantly, till thick. Chill.

Fold in pineapple, apple, celery, and the whipped cream. Pour into 2-quart refrigerator tray. Freeze firm. Cut in squares and trim with fans of apple slices.

Makes 10 to 12 servings.

Fruit Freeze, Oriental

1 3-ounce package cream cheese
3 tablespoons mayonnaise
1 tablespoon lemon juice
¼ teaspoon salt
½ cup chopped preserved kumquats
½ cup dates, cut up
¼ cup quartered maraschino cherries
1 9-ounce can (1 cup) crushed pineapple, drained
2 tablespoons finely chopped candied ginger, if desired
1 cup heavy cream, whipped
¼ cup slivered blanched almonds, toasted

Soften cream cheese; blend in mayonnaise, lemon juice, and salt. Stir in fruits and ginger. Fold in whipped cream. Pour into refrigerator tray. Sprinkle almonds over top.

Freeze firm. Makes 6 to 8 servings.

Under red-cherry, green-grape trim Twenty-four Hour Salad is fluffy, full of fruit

Luscious Twenty-four Hour Salad is all ready ahead of time. Simply dress up; then serve to delighted guests.

FOR AN AUGUST AFTERNOON: MELON POLKA-DOT MOLD CIRCLED BY FRESH FRUITS, DRESSING,

COTTAGE CHEESE.

Capture the beauty of fruit in shimmery molded salads

Jewel-bright and filled with fruit, these sparkling gelatin salads are as good as they look. Each quivering bite is full of tangy delicate flavor. *And* these salads are hostess helpers—make them ahead; just unmold and trim at mealtime. Serve as hub of a summer meal or accompaniment for a winter one, with fresh fruit, chicken, ham.

Follow your fancy in molding salads. It's nice to own ring, melon, and individual molds. For different effects, chill salads in loaf pans, paper cups, fancy molds. Tip: To find out how much salad a mold will hold, measure the amount of water required to fill it.

Melon Polka-dot Mold

2 packages cherry-flavored gelatin
2 cups boiling water
1¾ cups cold water
3 tablespoons lemon juice, fresh, frozen, or canned
1 8-ounce package cream cheese
1½ cups cantaloupe, honeydew, or watermelon balls
⅔ cup pecan halves
½ cup sliced stuffed green olives

Dissolve gelatin in boiling water. Add cold water and lemon juice. Pour 1 cup gelatin mixture into 6½-cup ring mold. Chill till partially set.

Shape cream cheese in small balls (about 30). Alternate 9 cream-cheese balls with 9 melon balls in bottom of mold. Place pecan halves in gelatin clear around outer edge of bottom of mold. Chill firm.

Meanwhile chill remaining gelatin till partially set; add remaining cheese and melon balls, pecan halves, and the olive slices. Pour over first mixture and chill till firm.

Unmold and garnish with mint. Makes 8 to 10 servings.

Black-cherry Squares

2 1-pound cans (4 cups) pitted Bing cherries
⅓ cup lemon juice, fresh, frozen, or canned
1 package orange-flavored gelatin
¾ cup broken pecans
⅔ cup sliced stuffed green olives

Drain cherries; add enough of cherry syrup to lemon juice to make 1¾ cups liquid.

Heat to boiling; pour over gelatin and stir till dissolved. Chill till partially set. Add the cherries, nuts, and olives.

Pour into 10x6x1½-inch pan and chill till firm. Cut in squares and serve on lettuce.

Or chill in individual molds and unmold in pineapple rings. Makes 6 to 8 servings.

Fruity Holiday Wreath — happy combination of lime, lemonade, cherry ribbons.

Go festive with these layered fruit salads

Fruity Holiday Wreath

Lime layer:

1 package lime-flavored gelatin
2 cups boiling water
1 9-ounce can (1 cup) seedless white grapes, drained
½ cup chopped celery

Dissolve gelatin in boiling water. Chill till partially set. Add grapes and celery. Pour into 2-quart ring mold; chill till firm.

Lemonade layer:

1 envelope (1 tablespoon) unflavored gelatin
¼ cup cold water
1 cup boiling water
½ cup frozen lemonade concentrate*
½ cup mayonnaise or salad dressing

Soften gelatin in cold water; dissolve in boiling water. Add lemonade concentrate; blend

Five fruit flavors blend inside sparkling, colorful Pineapple-top Layers

in mayonnaise. Chill till partially set. Pour over lime layer; chill till firm.
*Use remainder of concentrate in Lemon Mayonnaise, page 134. Serve with salad.

Cherry layer:

1 1-pound can (2 cups) fruit cocktail
1 package cherry-flavored gelatin
1 cup boiling water

Drain fruit cocktail; reserve syrup, adding water to make 1 cup. Dissolve gelatin in boiling water, then add reserved fruit-cocktail syrup. Chill till partially set. Add fruit cocktail; pour over other layers; chill till firm.

Unmold on greens. Makes 12 servings.

Pineapple-top Layers

Pineapple-lime layer:

1 package lime-flavored gelatin
1 cup boiling water
1 9-ounce can (1 cup) sliced pineapple
2 tablespoons lemon juice

Dissolve gelatin in boiling water. Drain pineapple, reserving syrup. Add lemon juice to syrup and enough water to make 1 cup; add to dissolved gelatin. Chill till partially set.

Cut pineapple slices in thirds; arrange in an "S" design, as shown, in bottom of 10x5x 3-inch loaf pan. Pour small amount of gelatin mixture over pineapple; chill till set. Then add rest of gelatin mixture; chill till firm.

Lemon-cream cheese layer:

1 package lemon-flavored gelatin
1 cup boiling water
2 3-ounce packages cream cheese
⅓ cup mayonnaise

Dissolve gelatin in boiling water. Chill till thick. Then whip till light and fluffy. Blend softened cream cheese and mayonnaise; fold into gelatin. Pour mixture over lime layer; chill till firm.

Raspberry-banana layer:

1 package raspberry-flavored gelatin
2 cups boiling water
2 fully ripe bananas

Dissolve gelatin in boiling water. Slice bananas over lemon layer; pour dissolved gelatin over all. Chill till firm. Makes 12 servings.

Here's an ideal all-season salad, designed to serve the crowd. Bottom layer is raspberry gelatin, chock-full of ripe banana slices.

Lemon gelatin—whipped to a fluff, smoothed with cream cheese—makes the middle.

And to top it all off, the crowning, lime-flavored layer has built-in pineapple trim.

Polka-dot gelatin beauties with mixed fruit

Red-and-white Fruit Mold

1 1-pound can (2 cups) fruit cocktail
1 package raspberry- or strawberry-flavored gelatin

• • •

1 package lemon-flavored gelatin
1 cup boiling water
1 6-ounce can frozen lemonade concentrate
½ cup mayonnaise or salad dressing

Drain fruit cocktail, reserving syrup. Add water to syrup to make 2 cups. Heat 1 cup of mixture to boiling; add raspberry gelatin and stir to dissolve. Then add remaining syrup mixture.

Pour gelatin mixture into a 6½- or 7-cup mold, or pour equal amounts into individual molds. Chill till firm.

Meanwhile dissolve lemon gelatin in 1 cup boiling water; add lemonade concentrate. Blend in mayonnaise. Chill till partially set; then stir in fruit cocktail. Pour over first layer and chill till firm.

To match picture, unmold large salad on platter and circle with fruits, including Frosted Grapes. Tuck in mint. Pass a bowlful of Red-currant Dressing.

Unmold individual salads on rings of pineapple, if desired, and trim each with a ruffle of leaf lettuce.

For elegance, serve salads on platter centered with luscious, fruit-filled Honeydew Bowl. Pass muffins, toasted crackers.

tips ***To unmold gelatin perfectly—rinse platter, dip mold***

Before unmolding gelatin, rinse platter or plate with cold water so mold will slide on it.

To loosen mold, run tip of knife between gelatin and pan. Dip mold just to rim in warm water, for a few seconds. Place wet platter atop mold, hold tight, invert quickly. Lift off pan. Push mold with back of spatula, to center it.

Fluffy Fruit Mold is smooth and creamy, full of pineapple and grapes, whipped cream, and mayonnaise—salad and sweet dressing rolled into one. With fruit, it's a salad-dessert.

Honeydew Bowl: Chill a large honeydew melon. Cut off top, one-fourth of the way down. Scoop out seeds. Pare melon.

With round biscuit cutter, cut deep scallops around top of melon bowl (hold bottom of custard cup or glass against melon on inside as you press with cutter).

Coarsely dice melon left from scallops and top; mix with canned peach and pear slices and pineapple spears, seedless grapes.

Fill melon bowl with the mixed fruit. Trim with maraschino cherries and sprigs of mint. Pass Red-currant Dressing.

Fruited Ribbon Loaf

2 packages cherry- or raspberry-flavored gelatin
2 cups boiling water
2 cups cold water
¼ teaspoon salt

• • •

1 1-pound can (2 cups) fruits for salad, drained

• • •

3 tablespoons lemon juice, fresh, frozen, or canned

• • •

1 teaspoon grated lemon peel

Dissolve gelatin in boiling water. Add cold water and salt.

First layer: Arrange fruits for salad in a 9½x5x3-inch loaf pan. Carefully pour 1 cup gelatin mixture over. Chill till firm.

Second layer: Add lemon juice to remaining gelatin mixture. Measure 1 cup of this mixture; add lemon peel. Chill till partially set; beat with rotary or electric beater till light and fluffy. Pour over fruit layer; chill till firm.

Third layer: Chill remaining gelatin till thick; pour over whipped layer. Chill till firm. Unmold on platter and garnish with water cress. Makes 8 to 10 servings.

Fluffy Fruit Mold

¾ cup sugar
1 envelope (1 tablespoon) unflavored gelatin
¼ cup water
1 stiff-beaten egg white
1 cup heavy cream, whipped
¼ cup mayonnaise or salad dressing
1 9-ounce can (1 cup) pineapple tidbits, drained
½ cup green seedless grapes
½ cup broken California walnuts

Combine sugar and gelatin. Stir in water; bring just to boiling. Pour slowly over beaten egg white, beating until thick (about 5 minutes). Cool. Fold in whipped cream, then mayonnaise. Add pineapple tidbits, seedless grapes, and broken walnuts.

Pour into 1-quart mold. Chill till firm. Serve with assorted fruits. Serves 6 to 8.

Sparkling Red-and-white Fruit Mold is served two ways—bordered with fruits, centered with luscious Honeydew Bowl

Honeydew Bowl and individual salads

Red-currant Dressing

Single large mold with fresh fruit

Club Fruit-salad Squares

1 No. 2 can (2½ cups) pineapple tidbits
1 1-pound can (2 cups) pitted Royal Anne cherries
½ cup sugar
3 tablespoons cornstarch
¼ teaspoon salt
½ cup orange juice
1 slightly beaten egg
1 envelope (1 tablespoon) unflavored gelatin
¼ cup lemon juice

• • •

1 orange, pared and diced
1 cup sliced strawberries
¼ pound (2 cups) tiny marshmallows
½ cup broken pecans
1 cup heavy cream, whipped

Drain pineapple, reserving ½ cup syrup. Drain cherries, reserving ½ cup syrup. Combine sugar, cornstarch, and salt; stir in reserved syrups, orange juice. Cook over low heat, stirring constantly, till thick. Stir small amount of mixture into egg; return to hot mixture. Cook 1 minute; stir constantly.

Soften gelatin in lemon juice; dissolve in hot mixture. Chill till partially set.

Add fruits, marshmallows, and nuts. Fold in whipped cream. Pour into 11x7x1½-inch pan; chill till set. Cut in squares and top with whole strawberries. Makes 10 servings.

Rosy Fruit Molds with Cheese

1 No. 2 can sliced pineapple
1 1-pound can (2 cups) fruit cocktail
1 package raspberry-flavored gelatin
3 tablespoons lemon juice, fresh, frozen, or canned
¼ teaspoon almond extract

• • •

1 3-ounce package cream cheese
8 walnut halves

Drain pineapple and fruit cocktail; reserve syrups. Add enough water to mixed syrups to make 2 cups. Heat *1 cup* of liquid to boiling; pour over gelatin and stir till dissolved. Add remaining liquid, lemon juice, and almond extract; chill till partially set.

Cut cream cheese in 8 squares. Form each square into ball, around a walnut half. Place cheese balls in bottom of individual molds. Stir fruit cocktail into gelatin mixture. Pour over cheese balls. Chill till firm. Unmold on pineapple slices. Makes 8 servings.

Jellied Ambrosia

1 envelope (1 tablespoon) unflavored gelatin
¼ cup sugar
½ cup boiling water
1¼ cups orange juice
1 tablespoon lemon juice
1½ cups orange segments
1½ cups banana slices
¼ cup flaked coconut

Thoroughly mix gelatin and sugar; add boiling water, stirring till sugar and gelatin are dissolved. Add orange and lemon juice. Chill till partially set.

Then fold in oranges, bananas, and coconut. Pour into 1-quart mold. Chill till set.

Unmold on lettuce. Trim with banana slices and orange segments.

Makes 6 servings.

Fruity Ginger-ale Mold

1 package lemon-flavored gelatin
1 cup boiling water
Dash salt
1 small bottle ginger ale, chilled
1 unpared apple, cut in thin wedges
½ cup chopped pared apple
½ cup green seedless grapes
1 9-ounce can (1 cup) pineapple tidbits, drained

Dissolve gelatin in boiling water. Add salt, cool. Add ginger ale. Chill till partially set.

Arrange apple wedges in 5½-cup mold. Pour in a little of gelatin mixture. Chill quickly in freezing compartment till set. Add rest of ingredients to rest of gelatin mixture. Pour in mold. Chill firm. Serves 6 to 8.

Molded Cranberry Waldorfs

1 pint bottle (2 cups) cranberry-juice cocktail
1 package lemon-flavored gelatin
¼ teaspoon salt
1 cup chopped unpared apple
½ cup chopped celery
¼ cup broken California walnuts

Heat *1 cup* of cranberry-juice cocktail just to boiling. Dissolve gelatin in it. Add rest of juice and salt. Chill till partially set.

Stir in apple, celery, and nuts. Pour into 6 individual molds. Chill till firm.

Cinnamon Applesauce Salad

2 packages lemon-flavored gelatin
½ cup red cinnamon candies
3 cups boiling water
2 cups unsweetened applesauce
1 tablespoon lemon juice
½ cup broken California walnuts
2 3-ounce packages cream cheese, softened
¼ cup milk or light cream
2 tablespoons salad dressing

Dissolve gelatin and candy in boiling water. Stir in applesauce, lemon juice, and a dash salt. Chill till partially set. Add nuts. Pour into 8x8x2-inch pan. Blend remaining ingredients; spoon atop; swirl through salad to marble. Chill firm. Cut in 9 squares.

Double Apple Salad

1 package lemon-flavored gelatin
2 cups boiling cider or apple juice
½ teaspoon salt
2 tart medium apples
¼ cup diced celery
⅓ cup coarsely broken walnuts
2 tablespoons diced pimiento

Dissolve gelatin in cider. Add salt. Chill till partially set. Cover bottom of 1-quart mold with thin layer of gelatin mixture. Cut one of the apples (unpared) in wedges and arrange in gelatin in mold; chill till firm.

Meanwhile, pare the other apple and cut in short sticks; add to the remaining gelatin along with remaining ingredients. Pour over firm gelatin in mold. Chill until firm.

Makes 4 to 6 servings.

Sweet Apple Ring

1 package lemon-flavored gelatin
1¾ cups boiling cider
½ teaspoon salt
1½ cups diced unpared apple
1 cup green seedless grapes
1 9-ounce can (1 cup) pineapple tidbits
8 to 10 marshmallows, cut in eighths

Dissolve gelatin in boiling cider and add salt. Chill till partially set. Add diced apple, grapes, pineapple tidbits, and marshmallows and pour into a 5-cup ring mold. Chill until set. Unmold on lettuce.

Makes 8 servings.

Shimmery cranberry and apple salads are planned to accent holiday turkey, fall meats

In tangy Cranberry Cups, zing of fresh cranberries and lemon juice blends with sweet fruit flavor of oranges and pineapple.

Walnuts and celery make the crunch; pineapple rings and tiny lettuce leaves are trim.

To match picture, mold in custard cups.

Cranberry Cups

1 9-ounce can (1 cup) crushed pineapple
1 No. 2½ can (3½ cups) pineapple slices
1 package cherry-flavored gelatin
¼ cup sugar
1 tablespoon lemon juice

• • •

1 cup ground fresh cranberries
1 small unpared orange, quartered, seeded, and ground
1 cup chopped celery
½ cup broken California walnuts

Drain both kinds of pineapple, reserving syrup. In saucepan, combine gelatin and sugar. Add water to reserved syrup to make 2 cups; add to gelatin mixture. Heat and stir till gelatin and sugar dissolve; add lemon juice. Chill till partially set.

Add ground fruits, crushed pineapple, celery, and nuts. Pour into 8 or 9 individual molds. Chill till firm. Unmold on the pineapple rings atop lettuce. Top with dollops of mayonnaise and tiny lettuce leaves, to match picture.

Apricots, grapefruit shine in gelatin

Grapefruit-Cheese Squares

2 1-pound cans (4 cups) grapefruit sections
2 packages lemon-flavored gelatin
1 8-ounce package cream cheese
2 tablespoons milk
½ cup chopped California walnuts
Maraschino cherries

Drain grapefruit and add enough water to the syrup to make 3½ cups. Heat *half* the syrup mixture to boiling; add to gelatin and stir till gelatin dissolves. Add remaining syrup mixture; cool.

Reserve best grapefruit segments (about half) for top layer; arrange remaining segments in bottom of 9x9x2-inch pan. Carefully pour *half* of gelatin mixture over grapefruit in pan; chill until firm.

Soften cream cheese; blend in milk and nuts. Then spread over gelatin layer to make "filling" for salad. Chill.

Meanwhile, chill remaining gelatin mixture till partially set. Arrange reserved grapefruit and the cherries on top of cheese, so each serving will have built-in trim. Carefully pour remaining gelatin mixture over top. Chill till set. Cut in squares and serve on leaf lettuce. Makes 9 to 12 servings.

Apple-Grapefruit Mold

1 1-pound can (2 cups) grapefruit
2 packages lime-flavored gelatin
2 cups boiling water
1½ cups diced unpared apple
½ cup broken California walnuts

Drain grapefruit, reserving juice. Dissolve gelatin in boiling water. Add grapefruit juice, plus enough water to make 1 cup. Chill till slightly thick.

Add apple, grapefruit, and nuts. Pour into 1-quart mold or 6 individual molds. Chill till set. Unmold and trim with walnut halves, if desired. Makes 6 servings.

Golden Apricot Molds

1 1-pound 14-ounce can (3½ cups) apricot halves
2 tablespoons vinegar
1 teaspoon whole cloves
4 inches stick cinnamon
1 package orange-flavored gelatin

Drain apricots, reserving syrup. Add vinegar and spices to syrup; bring to boiling. Simmer mixture for 10 minutes. Strain syrup and measure; add enough hot water to make 2 cups liquid. Pour over gelatin and

Try spicy Golden Apricot Molds

Juicy fruit, spice, and everything nice are what *these* sunny salads are made of!

They're shiny cups of orange gelatin, full of golden apricot halves, vinegar-and-spice tang.

Peeking out from under: slices of jellied cranberry sauce.

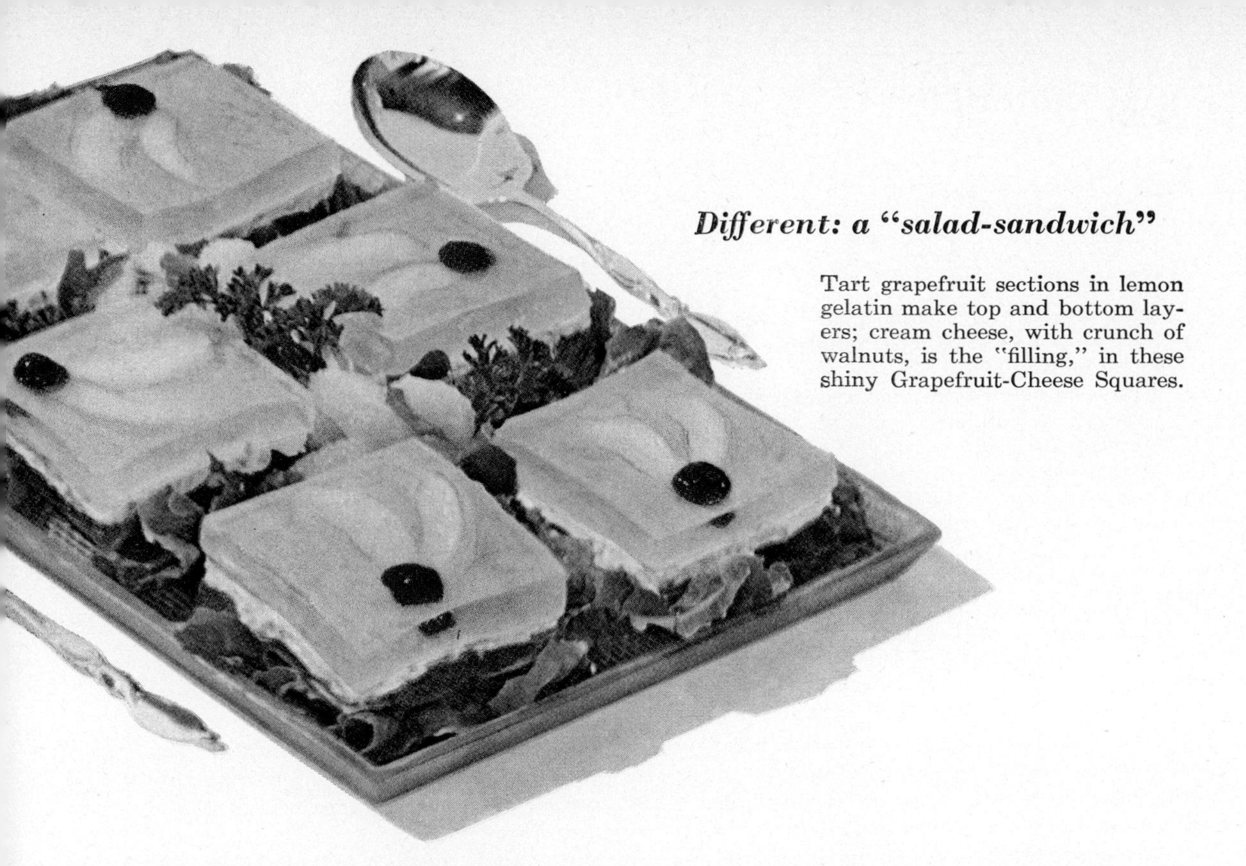

Different: a "salad-sandwich"

Tart grapefruit sections in lemon gelatin make top and bottom layers; cream cheese, with crunch of walnuts, is the "filling," in these shiny Grapefruit-Cheese Squares.

stir until dissolved. Place apricot halves in 8 individual molds and pour gelatin mixture over. Chill until firm.

Turn gelatin molds out on slices of canned jellied cranberry sauce atop lettuce to make an extra-good meat accompaniment. Serve with mayonnaise or Sweet Sour-cream Dressing. Makes 8 servings.

Sparkling Citrus Salad

1 9-ounce can (1 cup) crushed pineapple
1 1-pound can (2 cups) grapefruit sections
2 envelopes (2 tablespoons) unflavored gelatin
Dash salt
Dash paprika
⅓ cup broken pecans
2 small bottles (about 2 cups) ginger ale, chilled

Drain pineapple and grapefruit, reserving syrups. Sprinkle gelatin over reserved syrups in saucepan to soften, then heat and stir to dissolve. Remove from heat and stir in salt and paprika. Cool slightly. Stir in pineapple, grapefruit, and pecans. Chill till cold (but not long enough to start setting); then stir in the ginger ale.

Chill till partially set; pour into 1-quart mold. Chill till set. Unmold; trim with maraschino cherries if desired. Pass mayonnaise or fruit dressing. Makes 8 servings.

Avocado-Grapefruit Souffle

1 package lime-flavored gelatin
1 cup boiling water
½ cup cold water
1½ tablespoons lemon juice
½ cup mayonnaise
¼ teaspoon salt
2 tablespoons chopped green pepper
1 cup diced grapefruit sections, drained
½ cup mashed avocado pulp

Dissolve gelatin in boiling water. Stir in cold water, lemon juice, mayonnaise, and salt. Turn into freezing tray. Freeze 15 to 20 minutes, or till firm about 1 inch from edge but still soft in center.

Turn into bowl and whip with rotary beater until fluffy. Fold in green pepper, fruit. Pour into 1-quart mold; chill till firm (30 to 60 minutes). Makes 5 to 6 servings.

Use ice to get molded salad off to a flying start

Dissolve each package fruit-flavored gelatin in one cup *boiling* water; then add 8 to 12 ice cubes and stir constantly 2 to 3 minutes, till gelatin starts to thicken. Remove unmelted ice. Let stand 3 to 5 minutes; add fruit; chill firm.

Pear Salad Ring

1 No. 2½ can (3½ cups) pear halves
1 package lemon-flavored gelatin
1 cup boiling water
2 tablespoons lemon juice, fresh, frozen, or canned
¼ teaspoon ginger
¼ teaspoon salt

• • •

¼ cup chopped California walnuts
1 3-ounce package cream cheese, softened

• • •

Thin strips green pepper

Drain pears, reserving 1 cup syrup. Dissolve gelatin in boiling water. Add reserved pear syrup, lemon juice, ginger, and salt; blend. Cool until partially set. Meanwhile stir nuts into cream cheese; shape in small balls, place one in center of each pear half.

Arrange pear halves in 6½-cup ring mold, cut side toward center. Place green-pepper strips between. Pour gelatin mixture over all. Chill until firm. Unmold; fill center with pimiento cottage cheese. Trim platter with fruits. Makes 8 servings.

Jellied Strawberry Cups

1 9-ounce can (1 cup) pineapple tidbits
1 cup sweetened halved strawberries
Boiling water
1 package strawberry-flavored gelatin
2 tablespoons lemon juice, fresh, frozen, or canned
Dash salt

• • •

Canned pineapple slices
Leaf lettuce
Whole strawberries

Drain pineapple, reserving ½ cup syrup. Drain sweetened berries (be careful not to mash them), and to the juice add enough boiling water to make 1 cup; pour over gelatin and stir to dissolve. Add pineapple syrup, lemon juice, and salt to gelatin mixture. Chill until partially set.

Gently stir in berries and pineapple tidbits. Pour into individual molds. Chill till set. Frame each pineapple slice with leaf lettuce; unmold salad atop. Garnish with whole berries. Pass bowl of mayonnaise or salad dressing. Makes 5 to 6 servings.

Pear Salad Ring tingles with subtle ginger flavor and green-pepper tang. Pears hide creamy cheese balls.

Cool green beauty

Here's a glamorous partner for a sliced-ham platter or fried chicken—Pineapple in Emerald Wreath.

Green grapes, pineapple-ring dividers shine out of luscious lime gelatin. Center bowl of mayonnaise.

Pineapple in Emerald Wreath

2 packages lime-flavored gelatin
2 cups boiling water
Dash salt
3 No. 1 flat cans pineapple slices
3 tablespoons lemon juice
1½ cups green seedless grapes

Dissolve gelatin in boiling water; add salt. Drain pineapple, reserving syrup. Add lemon juice to pineapple syrup, then add enough cold water to make 2 cups. Add syrup mixture to gelatin and chill till partially set. Arrange pineapple slices on edge, two together, at 6 intervals around 6½-cup ring mold. Place grapes between pineapple dividers. Pour gelatin over fruit. Chill till firm.

If the pineapple slices extend above gelatin, trim before unmolding.

Makes 6 to 8 servings.

Peach-Pineapple Ring

3 packages lemon-flavored gelatin
2 cups boiling water
1 No. 2½ can (3½ cups) peach halves
1 No. 2½ can (3½ cups) pineapple slices
½ cup (20) drained maraschino cherries

Dissolve gelatin in boiling water. Drain peaches and pineapple, reserving syrups. Combine syrups and add cold water to make 3 cups. Add syrup mixture to dissolved gelatin. Chill till partially set.

Alternate peach halves and cherries in bottom of 2½-quart ring mold. Halve pineapple slices and dip in gelatin; stand up (with cut edges down) around sides of mold, to make "scalloped" design. Place remaining cherries in centers of half-rings. Pour gelatin mixture over fruit. Chill till firm.

Makes 10 to 12 servings.

Pineapple-Rhubarb Mold

2 cups 1-inch slices fresh rhubarb
⅓ cup sugar
½ cup water

• • •

1 No. 2 can (2½ cups) pineapple tidbits
1 package strawberry-flavored gelatin
2 teaspoons lemon juice, fresh, frozen, or canned

Combine rhubarb, sugar, and water; cover and cook just till tender, about 5 minutes. Drain thoroughly, reserving syrup. Drain pineapple, reserving syrup also.

Combine the pineapple and rhubarb syrups and add water to make 1¾ cups. Heat to boiling; add to gelatin and stir to dissolve. Add lemon juice. Cool, then chill until partially set.

Fold in rhubarb and pineapple; pour into 1-quart mold. Chill until set. Unmold on salad greens. Makes 6 to 8 servings.

Green and Gold Salad

1 1-pound can (2 cups) gooseberries
2 packages lemon-flavored gelatin
½ cup sugar
2 cups orange juice
2 cups celery slices
½ cup broken California walnuts

Drain gooseberries, reserving syrup. Add water to syrup to make 1¾ cups. Heat *1 cup* of syrup mixture just to boiling. Pour over gelatin and sugar; stir to dissolve. Add remaining ¾ cup syrup mixture and orange juice. Chill till partially set.

Stir in gooseberries, celery, and nuts. Pour into 6x10x1½-inch baking dish. Chill till firm. Cut in squares and serve on lettuce. Trim with fans of orange segments, if desired. Makes 8 servings.

Vegetable salads

Could a carrot give a girl a curl? Fun to think so.

Can the lettuces and cabbages, ruddy tomatoes, the cukes and crisp peppers, little green onions and early radishes give your meals the beauty of sunshine, the rosy cheeks and fine tingle of fresh air? You bet. They can do *all* that.

A beautiful vegetable salad can make your meals so tempting to the fork that your family eats with real *enjoyment*—heady praise, indeed, for you, the cook. There's no easier, no more pleasurable way you can serve the ingredients for good health, a Come-on-World zest for living.

Master the favorites, and try some surprises

The salad to be expert on is the green salad. If you're a pinch of this n' that person, your dish! You can create a flavor magnificence that will keep them forever guessing. Not much for hocus pocus? We give exact measures. Take in the tips on pages 52 and 53.

Relish trays are beautifully easy. The trick's in having every bite crunchy; the fun's in arranging. You can be forthright or fancy. (All about that on pages 68 to 73.)

The homespun favorites—Potato Salad, Coleslaw, Perfection Salad, Sunshine Salad—those wonderful, good-eating salads that make the most trips 'round the table at picnics, harvest suppers, barbecues. Master these.

Surprises wait for you on every page. New tips, dips, dressings. Salads hot, salads cold; souffle salads, tangy aspics; salads for Dutch lunch and luncheon; salads for dinner. Mealtime can be year-round springtime!

Fresh, crunchy—vegetable salad parade

← No wonder Peter Rabbit ventured into our crisp salad garden! Everything's fresh as lettuce, crunchy as new cabbage.

At top, quick-n'-pretty relish tray pairs with Blue-cheese Dip. Next comes Cabbage-patch Coleslaw, then Salad Ensemble of Herbed Tomato Slices, Carrot-Olive Slaw, Relish Cottage Cheese. Perfection Molds and Deviled Eggs line up behind Peter. Carrot sticks are to dunk in Spring Garden Dip.

Subtly seasoned, quickly served, it's delicious

tossed green salad

First, put the garlic in!

Here's a trick for spreading subtle flavor through salad—crush garlic cloves into salt in bowl, with pestle.

Other ways: Rub cut end of garlic clove over bowl, or mince clove in garlic press and add to dressing.

Sometimes, awe guests by mixing dressing right in bowl before adding greens—twice as much oil as vinegar (guess), smidgen of mustard, dash of salt, freshly ground pepper.

Then break up lettuce

Break lettuce by hand in bite-size pieces—it looks fresher and prettier than lettuce cut with a knife.

For a treat, try salads with different greens—tiny heads of Bibb lettuce cut in quarters, sticks of French endive, crosswise slices of Chinese cabbage.

Add a little of the nippy greens—tender water cress, curly endive, escarole, or tiny spinach leaves.

Last, toss with dressing

Just before serving, pour on Italian or French dressing, bottled or "home-mixed." Use just enough to coat the greens. Add freshly ground pepper for zip, and a dash of salt.

At last minute gently toss in tomato wedges, other remaining ingredients. Or, arrange atop greens, and add dressing, toss at table.

And it's ready to serve, crisp, green, glistening! For a quick trim, top finished salad with red tomato wedges, green-pepper diamonds, sprigs of water cress. Serve immediately in individual salad bowls and pass thick buttered slices of warm French bread.

Green Salad, Family-style

½ head lettuce
¼ bunch curly endive
½ bunch water cress

• • •

2 tomatoes, cut in wedges
2 stalks celery, cut in sticks
6 radishes, sliced
3 green onions, chopped
½ green pepper, sliced

• • •

¼ cup French or cheese dressing*

Break lettuce in bowl; tear endive and water cress in small pieces. Arrange remaining vegetables on top. Pour dressing over and toss lightly. Makes 6 servings.

*See recipes for Creamy Roquefort Dressing and Blue-Cheese Topper on pages 68, 69.

For tidy "tossing," roll salad

Nary a leaf jumps bowl! With salad fork in left hand, spoon in right, go to bottom of bowl with spoon as you go up and over with fork.

Fork goes under, spoon over, till tossing is done.

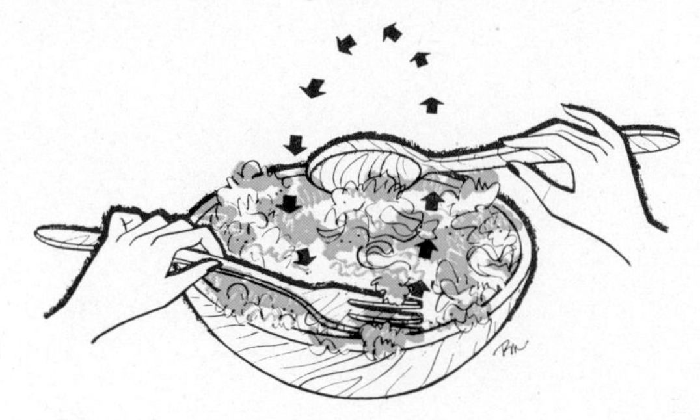

Choose from variety of **greens** for

Leaf lettuce tempts people and bunnies in early gardens →

Escarole's rich green is matched by lively flavor ↓

Lettuces, on striped board, await salad-maker and snappy dressing—bright green Bibb between lemons, delicate Boston above it; half a head of iceberg lettuce, a bunch of leafy romaine. All are good mixers, all gently crisp. ↓

↑ Curly endive looks lacy, tastes bracing

↑ Parsley joins salad in snips or as a fluffy bouquet

salad beauty

When you shop for salad-makings, you'll pick up firm head lettuce (iceberg) to chunk, cool, and crisp, into the salad bowl. And frilly leaf lettuce will tempt you—all it needs is a cool splash and the simplest of dressings, to remind you of spring. But slow down to an easy stroll now . . . other greens, beautiful, loaded with vitamins, can give you fresh, *new* salad-tossing fun.

For leaves to garnish or toss—curly leaf escarole, lacy-leaf endive; velvety Boston lettuce and bright, tender Bibb; "nut-flavored" romaine, fresh young spinach. For slicing in tossed salads—tangy French endive, tender Chinese celery. For slaws—red and green cabbage. For garnish *and* flavor—water cress, parsley, snappy chives and green onions, bright bitey radishes.

And don't forget beet tops, mustard and turnip greens, chunky celery, green pepper, tomatoes. Good hunting . . . *good* salad!

Green cabbage, crackly crisp for bowl of slaw

Chinese (or celery) cabbage slices into crunchy, juicy bites

Red cabbage in curly shreds brightens greens

Bill Hopkins

Water cress puts pep in your salad

For crispy greens, wash and dry—then store

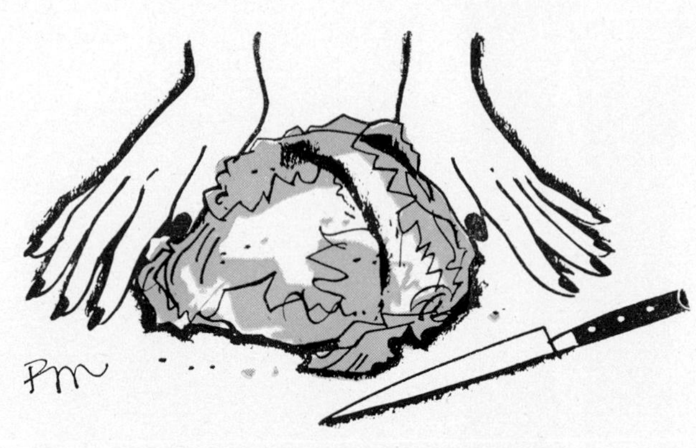

Lettuce cups from tight head

Remove lettuce cups from tight heads this way. Wash, core, and drain head.

Then turn it top down on a hard surface. Press down with palms of hands and wiggle it first one direction, then the other, to loosen.

Gently pull off cups. Store balance of head.

Give greens a cold shower

Discard discolored or wilted leaves. Rinse greens well under cold water, but don't soak. For lettuce cups, core head, then run water through core. Drain; gently peel off leaves.

Use paper or cloth towels, or wire basket to dry greens

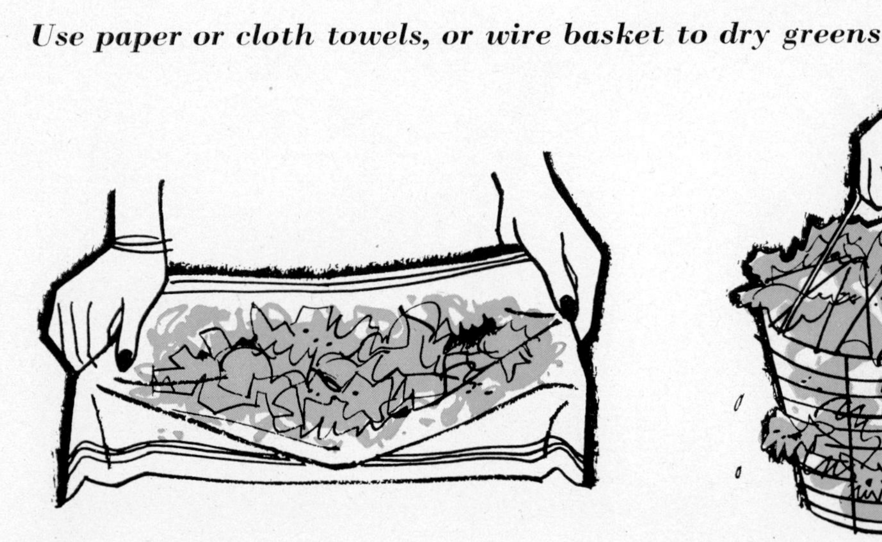

Drain or toss to dry . . .

Drain excess water from head lettuce on rack or on paper towels. Toss leafy greens like romaine, leaf lettuce, escarole and curly endive in a clean kitchen towel or in paper towels.

Salad dressing coats dry leaves evenly, but is diluted and runs off wet leaves.

or shake in wire basket

Another way to dry the fluffy greens is to shake or whirl them in a wire salad basket. (They won't bruise.)

Small greens like water cress and parsley are best patted dry with paper towels or a clean kitchen towel.

Crisper in refrigerator is tailored for storing vegetables and greens. If it's full, put greens in plastic bags or wrap in aluminum foil or saran wrapping before storing on lower shelves.

Store greens and salad vegetables in crisper or on lower shelves of refrigerator

Water cress and parsley keep fresh and green longest if stored in a covered jar in the refrigerator. Chives "store" at room temperature.

Buy them in a pot. Add soil, if desired; then set pot in warm water. Chives will grow for awhile; snip off as needed. Replace droopy ones.

Scrub vegetables, rub dry—so they are all ready to use

Use a vegetable brush to scrub carrots, celery, radishes, and green onions. Wash under cold water. Dispose of excess leaves and tops.

Wash tomatoes, green peppers, and cucumbers too. Store dry onions unwashed in bag in vegetable bin; clean when ready to use.

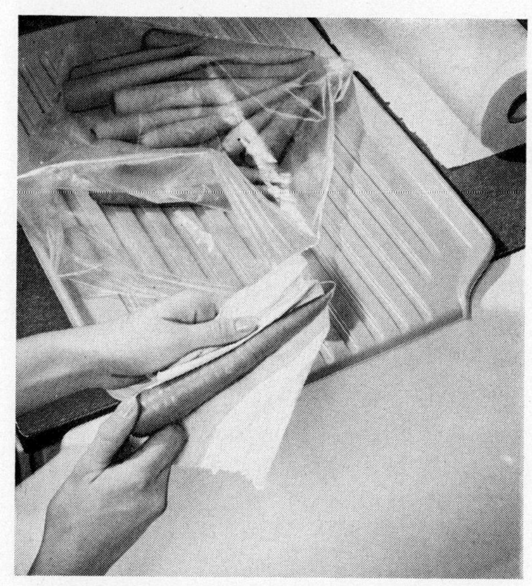

Wipe off scrubbed vegetables with paper towels. Wrap or bag each vegetable separately or place in crisper. (Wrap onions even for crisper.)

Slip paper towels into bags of greens; they will absorb any extra moisture left after drying or draining. Replace towels when damp.

Season wooden bowl, for salad flavor plus

Handy tools make salad-fixing quick—

Hostess *and* salad will be cool and fresh at serving time, when these hurry-up salad tools are on the job. Chores like chopping, grating, and slicing are out of the way in a jiffy.

A well-seasoned salad bowl is prized for another reason—you can't beat it for adding flavor, and prettiness, to a tossed salad.

Never soak the bowl—rinse it with lukewarm water—no soap—promptly wipe dry.

Some people are so fussy they won't even let a drop of water touch the bowl—they just wipe it out with dry paper towels. In time, garlic and salad seasonings will season the bowl to a connoisseur's taste.

Nice to have, too, are a set of salad tools for tossing and serving, and a pepper mill. Freshly ground pepper gives a special zing to any tossed green salad.

Versatile salad-maker—

Now it's busy slicing cucumber (add cool sour cream dressing; salad's ready). Other times it will grate, shred, "string," "waffle," chop, and pare vegetables for salads.

Five interchangeable rustproof cones of the helper do the work. Suction cups on the three "feet" keep unit anchored in place.

Perfect slices every time

. . . with this all-purpose slicer. Here it's tossing off shredded cabbage, after evenly slicing four other favorite salad vegetables.

It will also pare and slice fresh pineapple, "carve" roasts, slice ham, Bologna, other meats. The blade is stainless steel.

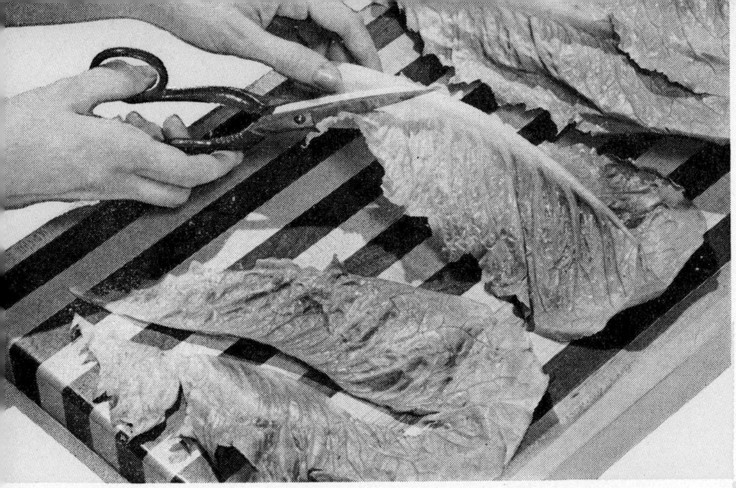

Scissors do the odd jobs

. . . like snipping the ribs from leaves of romaine. Or, put them to work cutting up green onion tops and chives, mincing parsley.

Use kitchen scissors too for halving grapes, clipping maraschino cherries into "flowers," cutting up marshmallows, dates.

Cutting board, chef's knife

. . . are a handy pair. This board is a special one. Little plastic bowl slides under cutout area so you can scoot cut-up vegetables and fruits off the working space.

Chef's knife is strong, sharp—just right for chopping vegetables for salads.

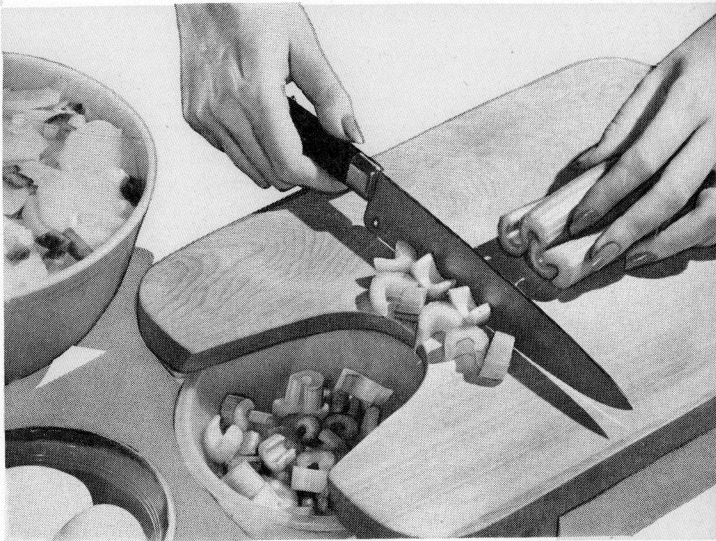

Complete salad "outfits"

Plastic twin-bowl set is for "tossing" salads. Built-in ring in the bottom of lower bowl is for the dressing. To toss, just fit the two bowls together and shake.

Other helps are wire baskets for rinsing salad greens, tong and scissor servers, cutting board, and curved-to-fit-hand knife.

Shredder for every purpose

This spacesaving shredder set includes three different-size plates, so it is possible to "custom-shred" any food you wish—carrots, cabbage, cucumbers, and cheese.

To use, prop up shredder on cutting board, or in bowl, or lay across bowl.

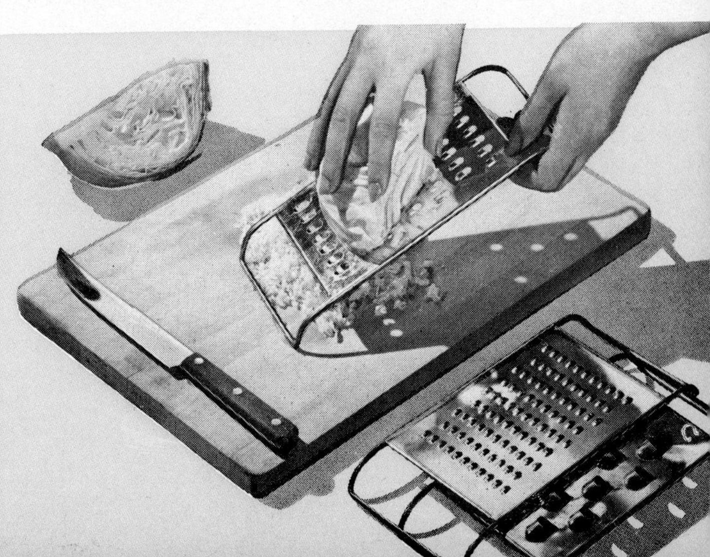

Favorite salad bowls

Spring Salad Bowl

1 bunch leaf lettuce, bite-size pieces
½ bunch water cress
1½ cups tiny spinach leaves
24 carrot curls
4 green onions with tops, chopped
12 pitted ripe olives (optional)
12 blanched almonds, toasted (optional)

Combine greens, carrot curls, and onions. Stuff olives with almonds and add. Toss with Italian dressing. Makes 6 servings.

Fall Salad Bowl

1 bunch romaine
4 heads Bibb lettuce
3 tomatoes, cut in wedges
1 cucumber, sliced
2 avocados, sliced
2 hard-cooked eggs, sliced

Line bowl with romaine. Separate Bibb lettuce in leaves and add. Arrange tomato wedges, cucumber, avocado, and egg slices in bowl. Toss with Italian dressing or French mayonnaise, or serve with Thousand Island Dressing. Makes 8 to 10 servings.

tips ***Give pretty new look to celery slices***

For attractive celery slices, cut on bias as shown. Why not save time by slicing several stalks at once?

Summer Salad Bowl

Leaf lettuce
½ head lettuce, in bite-size pieces
1 cup bias-cut celery slices
1 cup sliced radishes
2 cups sliced raw cauliflower
1 green pepper, thinly sliced
½ teaspoon salt
⅓ cup crumbled blue cheese
Italian dressing

Line bowl with leaf lettuce. Arrange head lettuce and remaining vegetables in bowl; add salt. Sprinkle blue cheese over. At table, pour dressing over, toss.

Makes 6 to 8 servings.

(An ice "jacket" keeps the crunch in summer salads. Fit two bowls of different sizes together and pack crushed ice in between—works with individual salad bowls and fruit cups, too.)

Winter Salad Bowl

¼ bunch curly endive
1 small head lettuce
2 oranges, pared and sliced*
½ mild white onion, sliced and separated in rings
Garlic dressing

Tear endive and head lettuce in bite-size pieces. Arrange orange slices and onion rings atop greens. Toss at table with dressing.

Makes 6 to 8 servings.

*Or substitute fresh orange sections, canned mandarin orange segments, if desired.

Here's a salad for each season

Spring Bowl, crunchy with carrot curls and almonds, tops page. Next is Summer Bowl on ice, then rich crispy Fall Bowl. Oranges, onion, endive make Winter Bowl piquant, pretty. →

Allen Snook, Inc.

Avocado-Shrimp Bowls

½ head lettuce
½ bunch curly endive
½ bunch water cress
1 cup cleaned cooked or canned shrimp, drained
3 hard-cooked eggs, sliced
1 avocado, sliced

Break up lettuce in bite-size pieces. Tear endive and water cress in small pieces. Arrange mixed greens in individual salad bowls.

Top with shrimp, egg slices, and avocado. Pass clear French dressing. Makes 6 servings.

Cheese-Anchovy Bowl: Omit shrimp, eggs, and avocado. Substitute ¾ cup Swiss cheese, cut in strips, and one 2-ounce can anchovy fillets. Toss in large bowl with Italian dressing.

Water Cress with Saffron Topper

1 tablespoon vinegar
¼ teaspoon saffron, crushed
¼ cup mayonnaise
1 3-ounce package cream cheese
3 to 4 cups (2 bunches) water cress, with stems cut short
¾ cup thinly sliced celery

Heat vinegar in cup or spoon; add saffron and let stand 5 minutes. Blend into mayonnaise; let mixture stand at room temperature at least 2 hours. Then soften *half* the cream cheese and blend with mayonnaise mixture, to make dressing.

Cut remainder of cream cheese in ¼-inch cubes and mix with water cress and celery in bowl. Pour dressing over.

Season to taste with salt and pepper. Toss lightly and serve. Makes 4 to 6 servings.

tips ***Walnut "croutons" add delicious crunch***

Melt 2 tablespoons butter in skillet; add ½ teaspoon salt or garlic salt. Butter-brown ½ cup coarsely broken walnuts over medium heat, stirring constantly. Add salad dressing and browned nuts to greens, and toss.

Greens with Tomato Topper

1 large firm tomato, peeled, diced fine
2 tablespoons sliced green onions
¼ pound Cheddar cheese, cut in thin strips
⅓ cup clear French dressing
Leaf or Bibb lettuce
Water cress or curly endive

Combine tomato, onions, cheese, and French dressing. Line individual bowls with lettuce, sprigs of water cress. Spoon tomato mixture atop. Pass extra dressing.

Makes 6 servings.

Toss in extra tidbits for variety—they give flavor

How to make croutons

Leave crusts on bread slices. Cut bread into tiny cubes. Toast in slow oven, stirring frequently, till dry and golden brown. Melt butter in skillet with a peeled clove of garlic. Take out garlic when it is golden brown. Add croutons; toss till they are butter-coated. Sprinkle over green salad.

Store a supply of croutons in a covered jar in the refrigerator. Heat them just before using.

French Green Salad

Crisp lettuce
Water cress
Tender spinach leaves
Green celery tops
Cucumber slices
Chopped green onions
Clear French dressing

Rub salad bowl with peeled garlic clove. Break equal parts of each chilled green into bowl. Add cucumber and onion. Chill.

Just before serving, pour French dressing over. Sprinkle with salt and freshly ground pepper. Toss lightly until leaves are coated and glistening. Garnish with tomato and radish slices, if desired.

Pennsylvania-Dutch Lettuce

5 slices bacon, diced

• • •

1 beaten egg
¼ cup minced onion
2 tablespoons sugar
½ teaspoon salt
⅓ cup vinegar
2 tablespoons water

• • •

1 bunch leaf lettuce

Cook bacon till crisp. Combine remaining ingredients except the lettuce; add to bacon. Heat just to boiling, stirring constantly. Tear lettuce into bowl; pour hot dressing over and toss lightly. Makes 4 servings.

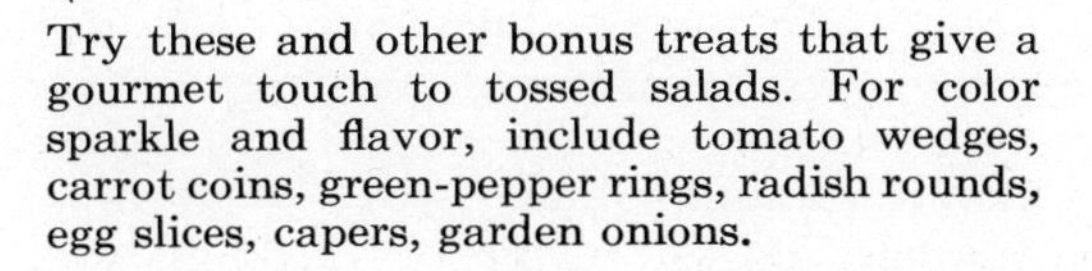

Try these and other bonus treats that give a gourmet touch to tossed salads. For color sparkle and flavor, include tomato wedges, carrot coins, green-pepper rings, radish rounds, egg slices, capers, garden onions.

Spinach Salad Bowl

6 cups shredded fresh spinach
1½ cups sliced radishes
¾ cup sliced green onions
Salt
½ cup Tomato Soup Dressing (page 131)

Arrange spinach, radishes, and onions in salad bowl; sprinkle with salt; pour dressing over. Toss together lightly.

Makes 6 servings.

Hot Spinach-Lettuce Toss

2 cups torn leaf lettuce
1 cup torn fresh spinach
¼ cup diced celery
1 tablespoon chopped green onion

• • •

5 slices bacon

• • •

¼ cup bacon drippings
¼ cup vinegar
2 tablespoons crumbled blue cheese
2 tablespoons sugar
½ teaspoon salt
½ teaspoon Worcestershire sauce

Combine vegetables in bowl. Cook bacon till crisp; drain on paper towels. Crumble bacon and add to salad. Combine remaining ingredients and pour over all. Toss lightly. Makes 6 servings.

Lettuce Toss with Hot Bacon Dressing

4 strips bacon, diced

• • •

4 cups leaf lettuce
1 large tomato, diced
¼ cup green-onion slices
½ teaspoon salt
½ teaspoon oregano
¼ teaspoon pepper

• • •

2 tablespoons vinegar

Fry bacon till crisp; drain, reserving 1 tablespoon fat. Meanwhile tear lettuce into bowl; add tomato and onion. Sprinkle greens with seasonings.

Combine vinegar and 1 tablespoon bacon fat; bring to boil. Pour over salad, tossing lightly to mix. Crumble bacon over top of salad. Serve immediately.

Makes 6 servings.

Group vegetables on a platter; let each

Meal-on-a-Platter

3 cups drained cooked or canned whole green beans
1½ cups drained cooked or canned peas
1 cup garlic dressing

• • •

1 12-ounce carton (1½ cups) large-curd cream-style cottage cheese
Chives or parsley

• • •

1 head lettuce
12 celery fans (page 70)
12 carrot curls (page 71)
1 12-ounce can luncheon meat, cut in thin strips
Pimiento strips
1 hard-cooked egg, sliced

Place beans and peas in separate dishes and pour garlic dressing over. Chill about 2 hours, turning occasionally. Drain.

Center platter with bowl of cottage cheese flecked with snipped chives. Arrange 4 large lettuce cups on platter; fill one each with peas, celery fans, carrot curls, and strips of luncheon meat.

Arrange beans in four bundles between lettuce cups; trim with pimiento. Pass extra dressing. Makes 6 servings.

Meal-on-a-Platter—nippy beans and peas, meat, eggs, and chive-flecked cottage cheese team up with crunchy celery and carrot curls.

Three-salad Ensemble

Arrange 3 large lettuce cups in shallow salad bowl. Fill one each with Herbed Tomato Slices, Relish Cottage Cheese, and Carrot-Olive Slaw (page 75).

To match picture on page 50, tuck parsley sprigs and thin slices of cucumber between lettuce cups. Pass cruet of French dressing. Makes 6 servings.

Herbed Tomato Slices:

⅓ cup salad oil
2 tablespoons wine vinegar with tarragon
Few leaves fresh thyme and marjoram, or ¼ teaspoon each of dried
½ teaspoon salt
Dash coarse black pepper
3 tomatoes, peeled and sliced

Combine first 5 ingredients. Place tomatoes in shallow bowl. Pour dressing over. Chill 2 to 3 hours, occasionally spooning dressing over tomatoes. Drain.

Relish Cottage Cheese:

1 12-ounce carton (1½ cups) large-curd cream-style cottage cheese, drained
2 tablespoons chopped green onions or chives
2 tablespoons chopped green pepper
2 tablespoons chopped pimiento
2 teaspoons prepared horseradish
¼ teaspoon salt

Combine ingredients. Keep chilled.

Supper Salad Wheel

Cook a variety of vegetables just till done, then pour oil-vinegar-style French or garlic dressing over each; chill about 2 hours, turning vegetables occasionally. Drain.

We show peas, green beans, baby Limas, and carrots arranged in separate dishes on Lazy Susan, with whole marinated cauliflower in center. Top cauliflower with Curried Chutney Dressing.

Arrange tomato and onion slices in one dish, pepper strips and pimiento in another.

Curried Chutney Dressing: Combine ¾ cup mayonnaise or salad dressing, 2 tablespoons chopped chutney, and ½ teaspoon curry powder. Top with pimiento diamonds.

guest help himself

Perfect to spark a buffet table—
whole-meal trays of salad vegetables,
some marinated, some crispy-fresh;
with hearty extras—meat, cheese

Supper Salad Wheel

Lazy Susan brimming with colorful vegetables teams up with Sesame Wedges, iced tea. Bright topper is Curried Chutney Dressing. Good!

Green Bean Bundles

Drain one 1-pound can green beans. Chill in 1/4 cup garlic dressing several hours. Drain and wrap bundles of beans in thin-sliced cold cuts. Arrange on Garden Tray or salad plates. Makes 4 to 6 servings.

Tangy Ripe Olives

Combine 1/3 cup wine vinegar, 1 1/3 cups salad oil, 4 cloves of garlic, minced.

Pour over one 10-ounce jar drained ripe olives. Chill several hours or overnight. Drain and sprinkle with minced parsley or chives. Serve in center of salad platter.

Asparagus Supper Plate shows off marinated asparagus, young carrots, and green Limas. For contrast—celery fans, ham, egg slices.

For porch picnic or special supper, these colorful platters are salad *and* vegetable

Garden Tray

Round-the-clock, arrange radishes, carrot curls, stuffed celery; Green Bean Bundles. Add cucumber sticks, olives, sliced cheese.

Back-yard Buffet

Cut whole tomatoes into stars. Turn stem end down; cut each one *not quite through* in 6 equal sections; spread apart. Sprinkle with salt. Top with sprigs of parsley and group on ruffles of lettuce in center of a large tray or Lazy Susan.

Group choice of fillings in dishes on both ends of tray. Offer Egg Salad, Crab-meat Salad, Guacamole (see tomato filling recipes, pages 80 through 83), chive cottage cheese, and mayonnaise.

Pass relishes, toasted coney buns, and cold milk. For dessert, bring out ice-cream sundaes and a plateful of crunchy cookies.

Use your slicer-shredder-grater to whip out Suit-yourself Salad—sliced raw beets and cucumbers, cabbage and carrot slaw. Add cauliflowerets, olives; pass bottled dressings.

Salad Star makes simple, luscious buffet service

Chunky slices of tomato, cucumber, turnip, and green pepper, forming the "star," are turned on edge like cart wheels, an idea from Jackson Lake Lodge near Moran, Wyoming.

Trim with green onions, gherkins, green and ripe olives, radish roses.

What could be more elegant than this Glamor Garden in a silver bowl?

Fluffy lettuce heart and wedges, zigzag cucumber cuts, and tomatoes nestle in greens. Pass dressing.

In a hurry? Try these jiffy salads

Try your hand at easy relish fix-ups

Go elegant just this quickly: Pipe pineapple-flavored cream cheese through pastry tube into chilled 4-inch celery sticks. Arrange with stuffed green olives; tuck in celery leaves. Salad's ready!

For an Italian-style meal, here's a quickie antipasto tray. (Everything comes ready-to-serve.) Fill a Lazy Susan with spiced artichoke hearts, Italian-style mild Tuscan salad peppers, pickled peppers (very hot), sweet red-pepper halves, olives, paper-thin pepperoni slices, salami roll-ups.

Tomato Slices a la Roquefort

Tomato-slice line-up calls for trim of green-onion circles and parsley fluffs, cheesy topper for accent.

Creamy Roquefort Dressing: Combine 1 cup mayonnaise, 1 tablespoon lemon juice, and 1 cup light cream. Crumble ½ pound Roquefort cheese into the mixture. Mix well and serve with tomatoes, greens. Makes about 3 cups of dressing.

Tomato-flower Salad is ready for the table as soon as you cut and arrange tomato wedges, and trim.

Cut a plump, red-ripe tomato in eighths as petals. Arrange wedges, cut side up, in circle on plate. Slice a crisscross in a small golden tomato. Place it in center of red wedges. Trim by tucking sprigs of curly endive in center of golden tomato and around red wedges. Pass Thousand Island Dressing.

Tomato-Pepper Chunk Salad is quick to fix ahead. Chill 3 cups diced tomato and 2 cups bite-size squares of green pepper in ¼ cup Italian dressing, an hour or more. Stir up and serve. Makes 4 to 6 servings.

Lightning-fast salad—Gourmet Lettuce Wedges

Start this speedy salad by cutting a chilled head of lettuce in wedges. Then spoon on this luscious creamy dressing, full of cheese:

Blue-Cheese Topper: Blend two 3-ounce packages cream cheese and 3 ounces (¾ cup) crumbled blue cheese. Stir in light cream till dressing is of consistency desired.

Chilly crisp salad platter is party-pretty and tasty

It takes just a few minutes to fix a gay salad platter, especially if you have a slicer or all-purpose tool to help.

For this platter, run carrots quickly through slicer, then arrange a golden mound on greens. Add snowy cauliflowerets, canned julienne-style beets. Tuck in some parsley sprigs. Pass French dressing, and a bowl of green onions, rosy radishes.

Another colorful platter is shown on page 50. Each person makes his own salad by choosing between leaves of Boston lettuce, cucumber and green-pepper slices, tomato wedges, cauliflowerets, radish roses, and carrot curls. Pass cheese topper.

Baskets of crispness

Rabbit food's served in pottery bunny baskets. One holds waffled carrot and celery sticks. The other is poked full of cucumber sticks and lettuce rolls.

You can roll leaf lettuce around sticks of cheese, ham, or carrot. Garnish with parsley.

These skip-the-fork salads are at home everywhere. Tuck sticks of carrot and celery into lunch boxes; dress up a fancy-dinner table with curls of the same; use them for garnishes.

Some relish fix-ups take a little time, others are clock racers. We give both.

Tip: To keep the crunch in relishes, chill well before serving, and, if desired, heap on crushed ice to bring to the table.

Celery Fans are a pretty variation of celery sticks. Cut tender celery stalks in 3- or 4-inch lengths. Make parallel cuts close together from one end *almost* to the other. Or slit both ends almost to the center. (To make fans that curl on top *and* bottom sides, make another cut crosswise through strips, to split each one in two.) Chill in ice water till strips curl.

Radish Accordions

Cut long radishes *not quite through* in 10 to 12 narrow slices. Chill in ice water so slices will fan out, accordion-style.

Slip into plastic bag and refrigerate till ready to use for relish or trim.

Serve relishes—crispy pickup salads

Plain as a row of cucumber sticks, fancy as artichoke leaves and lemon sauce—relishes are colorful, easy to serve, and good to eat

Traditional relishes

Here are carrot curls on ice, celery sticks and radish roses, cauliflowerets and ripe olives.

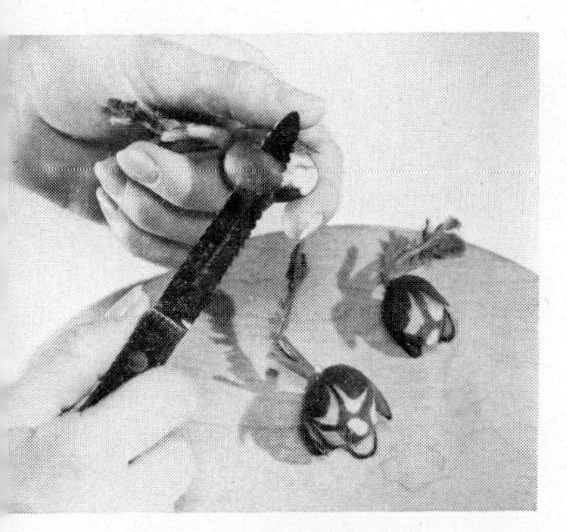

Perky Radish Roses

Cut off root, then cut four or five thin petals around radish, leaving bit of red between. Use grapefruit knife or tip of paring knife. Chill in ice water.

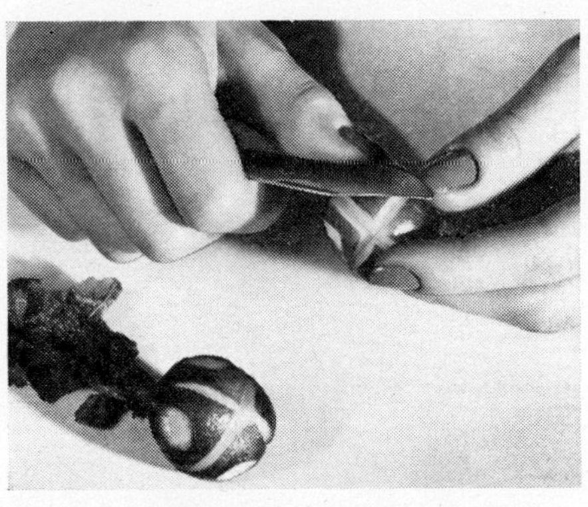

Red n' White Dominoes

Cut radish at root end to make a deep X. Now slice off thin circle of red peel in center of each fourth. Leave on tops. Chill before serving. Perfect trim for card-party sandwich tray, child's plate.

Petaled Daisies

With tip of knife, mark six petals on radish, starting at root end. Then cut petals back from root end as shown. Leave on some green leaves for trim. Chill in ice water to open.

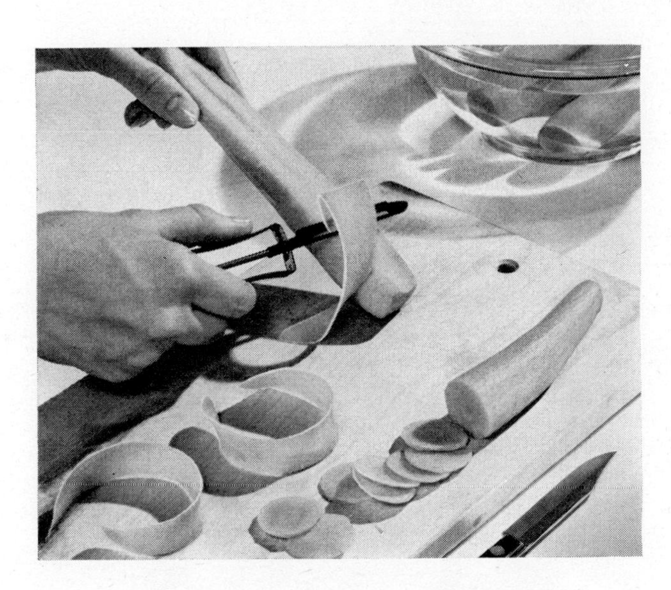

←

Pare carrots—now for the fun

First step for making carrot curls and zigzags is to cut thin lengthwise strips with parer. Rest carrot on board; pare *away* from you.

Carrot Crisps: With parer, slice carrot crosswise; drop thin circles in ice water. They crisp and ruffle prettily, take less time than curls.

Spear on toothpick; crisp →

Carrot Curls: Roll up long slices; toothpick to hold. Chill in ice water to crisp. Remove picks to serve. *Carrot Zigzags:* Spear slices accordion-style. Chill.

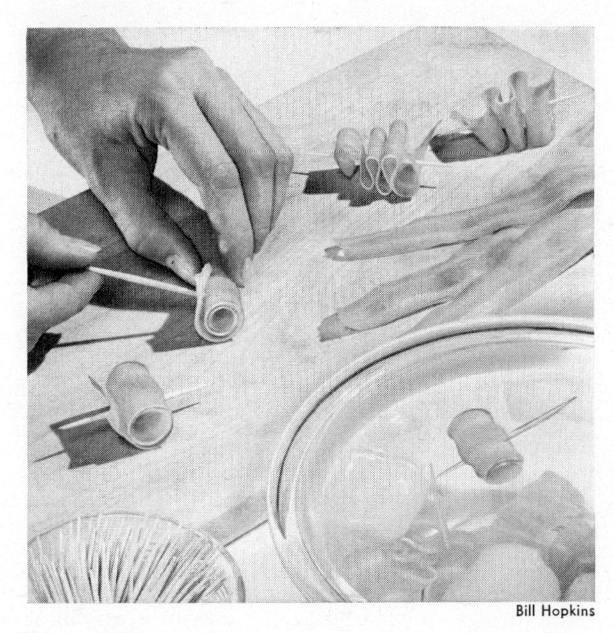

Bill Hopkins

←

Circular cut makes Corkscrews

To make carrot corkscrew, insert tip of short-bladed paring knife *almost* to center of carrot, at slight angle; rotate carrot slowly so it's cut into spiral. Deepen cut if necessary to make corkscrew flexible. Chill to open.

Relish spiral and artichoke bowl deck centerpiece tray

Swing row of tomato and onion slices halfway around tray; complete spiral with row of cauliflowerets, green-pepper rings, parsley, Carrot Corkscrews (page 71).
Center tray with radish-trimmed artichoke. To fix it, wash; then cut off stem, 1 inch of top, and sharp leaf tips. Brush cut edges with lemon juice. Place in small amount boiling salted water. Cover; simmer 25 minutes or till a leaf pulls out easily. Drain; remove center leaves, choke. Chill. Fill with Lemon Mayonnaise.

Posy Basket Salad doubles as a favor—each guest rates his own

Combine shredded lettuce, celery slices, thin cucumber slices, diced green pepper, and tomato wedges; toss with blue-cheese dressing. Line individual salad bowls with lettuce cups. Fill with the salad.
Cut a green pepper in ⅜-inch rings. Slit each ring to make strip and push a toothpick in each end as an extension and to give firmness. Insert in lettuce cup as basket handle. Tuck in a few Carrot Flowers on toothpick stems. Serve.
Carrot Flowers: Choose fat carrots. Cut out four shallow wedges full length of each carrot. Then slice carrot crosswise in thin rounds. Chill in ice water to cup or curl. Stick on green toothpicks.

Arrange finger salads in unusual ways; pass a dip or crackers

Dunking fans will cheer radish accordions, carrot curls, and celery sticks for dipping in well-seasoned cream cheese. Baked-ham strips and tiny sweet pickles are go-withs.

Crunchy sticks of French endive, cucumber, and celery "sprout" from pretty glass bowl — built-in chiller full of crushed ice keeps them daisy fresh. Wreath of bright green water cress makes a frilly springlike trim.

Palette-shaped bowl holds ripe olives, green onions, celery, and tomato wedges with cucumber. Cornucopias are salami slices toothpicked around cheese sticks.

Confetti Corn Relish

1 12-ounce can (1½ cups) whole-kernel corn, drained
¼ cup pickle relish
2 tablespoons chopped green pepper
1 tablespoon minced onion
1 tablespoon chopped pimiento
¼ teaspoon salt
2 tablespoons clear French dressing

Combine all ingredients. Chill. Serve on vegetable relish tray. Makes 1½ cups.

Fresh Cucumber Relish

Put three medium cucumbers through food chopper (medium-fine blade); drain. Add ¼ cup ground onion, ½ teaspoon pepper, 1½ teaspoons salt, ¼ cup cider vinegar, and 1 teaspoon dill seed. Mix well.

Chill in refrigerator several days to blend flavors. Makes 2 cups. Serve on salad tray.

Relish tray suggestions

Vary fillings for Stuffed Celery Sticks. Try cream cheese with drained crushed pineapple; pimiento cheese and chopped ripe olives; or mashed avocado seasoned with lemon juice, salt, and grated onion.

Make Beet Roses from canned pickled beets. Cut thin slices from bases so they will stand up. Then cut crisscross in top, cutting *almost* to bottom, of each one. Pipe softened cream cheese in the openings.

Counter-top relish chiller —

Fix relishes ahead. Then, if refrigerator's jammed, dip paper towels in ice water; wring, spread over relishes.

They stay crisp, pert during busy half-hour before dinner.

Asparagus Supper Salad—tasty

Here's a super choice for luncheon, or an excellent go-with-supper salad. Waist-line watchers will especially appreciate this treat; it's low in calories!

Chill cooked or canned asparagus. Arrange the tender green spears on a nest of lettuce. Add hard-cooked egg slices and strips of pimiento for flavor and color. Serve with Peppy Tomato Dressing— also a favorite with dieters.

Another asparagus salad idea: Cooked asparagus cuts (1-inch lengths) and slices of hard-cooked egg molded in Tomato Aspic.

Feature vegetables in dinner salads

Asparagus-fan Salad

1 cup French dressing
1 hard-cooked egg, chopped
2 tablespoons minced onion
2 teaspoons chopped parsley

• • •

Leaf lettuce
Chilled cooked asparagus, drained
Radish slices

Combine French dressing, egg, onion, and parsley for dressing. Line individual salad plates with leaf lettuce. On each one, arrange 4 to 6 asparagus spears in a fan shape, as shown on opposite page.

Tuck rows of radish slices between tips of asparagus spears. Garnish each salad with a juicy wedge of lemon and a radish rose, if desired. Pass a bowl of the dressing.

Hot Bean Salad

1 1-pound can (2 cups) kidney beans, drained
1 cup thinly sliced celery
¼ pound sharp process American cheese, diced (¾ cup)
⅓ cup chopped sweet pickle
¼ cup thinly sliced green onions
½ teaspoon salt
½ cup salad dressing or mayonnaise

• • •

⅓ cup rich-round-cracker crumbs

Combine all ingredients except the crumbs; toss lightly, spoon into four 8-ounce or six 5-ounce bakers or custard cups. Sprinkle crumbs atop. Bake in very hot oven (450°) 10 minutes or till bubbly. Garnish each with crisp bacon curl. Makes 4 to 6 servings.

Old-time Kidney-bean Salad

1 1-pound can (2 cups) kidney beans, drained
1½ cups chopped celery
½ cup chopped sweet pickle
¼ cup salad oil
1 tablespoon chopped onion
2 hard-cooked eggs, chopped
2 tablespoons vinegar
1 tablespoon pickle liquid
1 teaspoon salt
1½ teaspoons prepared mustard

Combine all ingredients. Toss lightly. Trim with egg slices. Makes 6 servings.

Carrot-Olive Slaw

¼ cup salad oil
2 tablespoons vinegar
1½ to 2 tablespoons sugar
¾ teaspoon salt
Dash pepper
• • •
3 cups shredded carrots
Ripe olive halves

Combine first 5 ingredients and toss lightly with carrots. Chill. Garnish with ripe-olive halves. (See page 50.) Makes 4 servings.

Peppy Beet Salad

1 1-pound can (2 cups) sliced or diced beets
½ cup vinegar
½ teaspoon cloves
½ teaspoon allspice
½ teaspoon cinnamon
¼ cup pickle relish
2 tablespoons chopped onion

Drain beets, reserving liquid. Add enough water to the liquid to make 1 cup; add vinegar and spices; bring to a boil. Add beets; remove from heat. Chill beets in liquid. Drain; add relish and onion; mix well. Top with onion rings. Makes 4 servings.

Caraway Coleslaw

½ cup dairy sour cream
2 tablespoons sugar
2 tablespoons vinegar
½ teaspoon salt
Dash pepper
2 teaspoons caraway seed
4 cups chilled, finely shredded cabbage

Combine all ingredients but cabbage; pour over cabbage. Mix lightly. Sprinkle with paprika, if desired. Makes 6 servings.

Greet the supper-table crowd with Hot Bean Salad! It's a medley of kidney beans, celery slices, and sharp cheese, plus sweet pickles and green onions. Those are crisp bacon curls on cracker-crumb top.

Pretty radish coins tuck in between asparagus spears in Asparagus-fan Salad. Serve with flavor pickup—a special French dressing. Garnish is lemon wedge.

Family favorite—coleslaw

Crisp from an hour on ice, slaw takes to dressings sweet or tart, turns special with crunchy extras, cabbage bowl

New-cabbage Slaw

2 cups shredded new cabbage
½ cup diced cucumber
½ cup diced celery
¼ cup chopped green pepper
1 teaspoon salt
¼ teaspoon paprika

• • •

½ cup salad dressing
2 tablespoons vinegar
1 teaspoon prepared mustard

Combine chilled vegetables, salt, and paprika. Combine remaining ingredients; pour over vegetables. Toss lightly. To match picture, serve in leafy cabbage bowl and trim with cucumber cuts. Makes 6 servings.

Coleslaw at its best

New-cabbage Slaw goes glamorous in this leafy bowl.

Festive variation of green slaw is Red-cabbage Toss. For a fruit and cabbage salad, try Apple-Pineapple Coleslaw.

Cabbage-patch Coleslaw

2 cups crisp shredded cabbage
½ cup chopped parsley
½ cup sliced green onions
2 to 3 tablespoons sugar
3 tablespoons vinegar
2 tablespoons salad oil
1 teaspoon salt

Combine vegetables. Blend rest of ingredients, stirring to dissolve sugar; pour over vegetables. Toss. Trim with sieved hard-cooked egg yolk, onion slices. Serves 6.

Red-cabbage Toss

2 cups finely shredded crisp red cabbage
1 cup sliced cauliflowerets
½ cup sliced celery
2 tablespoons finely chopped onion
1 tablespoon sugar
1 teaspoon salt
⅓ cup tarragon vinegar
3 tablespoons salad oil

Toss vegetables in bowl. Combine remaining ingredients; pour over vegetables. Toss. Chill 1 hour. Makes 4 to 5 servings.

Apple-Pineapple Coleslaw

3 cups shredded crisp cabbage
1 9-ounce can (1 cup) pineapple tidbits, drained
1 cup diced unpared apples
1 cup tiny marshmallows
½ cup chopped celery
½ cup mayonnaise

Combine, tossing till mayonnaise coats all ingredients. Serve in lettuce-lined bowl; trim with apple wedges. Serves 4 to 6.

Two ways with cabbage bowls

Select large green head of cabbage. Loosen outer green leaves, but don't break off. Cut remainder of head in eight sections *only halfway down.* Hollow out center, leaving shell of 6 to 8 leaves. Place upside down in ice water and allow to crisp. (Head opens to form bowl as on page 50.) Drain well. Shred center for slaw and refill "bowl."

Or, make bowl this way: Loosen crisp, curling outer leaves and spread out, petal fashion. With a sharp knife, hollow out center to within 1 inch of sides and bottom. Chop center to make slaw. (See finished bowl, opposite page.)

Sharp knife will cut even shreds of cabbage for coleslaw. Quarter the head; hold it firmly and slice.

If you like fine, juicy slaw, shred cabbage with knife first, then use three-edged chopper on it.

For fine, short shreds, use a shredder. Hold it on board or over bowl; push quarter-heads across it.

Calico Coleslaw

1½ cups finely shredded red cabbage
1½ cups finely shredded green cabbage
¼ cup minced onion
⅔ cup mayonnaise or salad dressing
1 tablespoon sugar
3 tablespoons vinegar
1 teaspoon salt
1 teaspoon celery seed

Combine chilled vegetables. Blend remaining ingredients, stirring to dissolve sugar. Pour over vegetables and toss. Makes 4 to 6 servings.

Hot Red Cabbage

2 tablespoons salad oil
½ medium head red cabbage (4 cups shredded)
2 medium apples, chopped
2 cups hot water
⅔ cup vinegar
3 tablespoons sugar
½ teaspoon salt

Heat oil; add rest of ingredients. Cook till apples are tender. Makes 6 servings.

tips ***Put frills on cucumber slices by fluting edges***

Run tines of fork down an unpared cucumber, all around. Then slice thin.

For extra-easy eating, cut scored cucumber in thirds, lengthwise, *almost to center*. Slice thin.

To trim molded salad, cut fluted slices in half; fan out; top with olive half.

Bacon-topped Skillet Slaw

4 slices bacon
¼ cup vinegar
1 teaspoon salt
1 tablespoon brown sugar
1 tablespoon finely chopped onion

• • •

4 cups (½ medium head) shredded cabbage
½ cup chopped parsley

Cook bacon till crisp; remove from the skillet and crumble. To fat in skillet, add vinegar, salt, sugar, and onion. Then add the crumbled bacon.

Heat dressing thoroughly; then remove from heat; add cabbage and parsley; toss. Makes 6 servings.

Cucumber Slices in Sour Cream

1 medium cucumber, sliced thin (2½ cups)
1 teaspoon salt

• • •

½ cup dairy sour cream
1 tablespoon vinegar
1 to 2 drops Tabasco sauce
2 tablespoons chopped chives
1 teaspoon dill seed
Dash pepper

Sprinkle sliced cucumber with salt; let stand about 30 minutes. Drain thoroughly. Combine sour cream, vinegar, Tabasco sauce, chives, dill seed, and pepper; pour over cucumbers. Chill well before serving, about 30 minutes.

To match picture, cluster radish roses atop cucumber slices. Garnish with minced parsley, radish rounds.

Serve as a tempting meat accompaniment or refreshing salad.

Makes 4 to 5 servings.

Mayonnaise Basket

Hollow 3-inch length of cucumber, leaving ¼-inch walls and base. Mark off lengthwise strips.

Pare every other strip down, almost to base (see center tray on opposite page). Then crisp in ice water.

Fill with mayonnaise and top with strips of pimiento. Makes attractive trim for salad tray.

Try summertime cucumber refreshers —guaranteed crisp, inviting

Temperatures drop degrees when these green-n'-white cucumber beauties come to table.

Choose from radish-topped Cucumber Slices in Sour Cream, Dutch Cucumbers with cherry tomatoes, Cool-as-a-Cucumber Salads circling Mayonnaise Basket. Or try Fluffy Cucumber Dressing, in hollowed-out cucumber boat. It's perfect with fruit, chicken, and seafood salads.

Spring Medley in Sour Cream

1 cup dairy sour cream
2 tablespoons lemon juice, fresh, frozen, or canned
1 teaspoon salt
¼ teaspoon dry mustard
• • •
1 cup sliced green onions and tops
1 cup sliced radishes
2 cups chopped cucumbers
Lettuce leaves

Thoroughly combine sour cream, lemon juice, salt, and mustard. Add onions, radishes, and cucumbers. Chill. Serve on lettuce. Makes 4 to 6 servings.

Cucumbers alone are good in this dressing. Serve with cold roast chicken, baked ham, or corned-beef hash.

Oriental Cucumber-Carrot Bowl

2 teaspoons salt
2 medium cucumbers, sliced paper-thin (2 cups)
• • •
2 cups shredded carrots
¼ teaspoon salt
½ cup sugar
½ cup white vinegar

Sprinkle 2 teaspoons salt over cucumbers. Chill thoroughly, 1 hour or longer. Drain in sieve, pressing with paper towels to remove as much moisture as possible. Sprinkle carrots with ¼ teaspoon salt.

Combine sugar and vinegar, stirring to dissolve sugar. Place drained cucumbers in one side of bowl, carrots in the other; pour vinegar mixture over. Chill at least one hour.

Before serving, drain off liquid; reserve to pass as dressing. Heap crispy cucumber in center of serving dish; circle with carrot.

Makes 5 servings.

(Salad stays crispy several days if covered and refrigerated. Leave dressing on.)

Dutch Cucumbers

Cut unpared cucumbers in *thin* slices. Sprinkle with salt, pepper, and sugar to taste. Barely cover with mixture of half vinegar and half iced water. Chill at least 1 hour or overnight.

Serve undrained. Trim with thinly sliced radishes. Or top with little cherry tomatoes and thin slices green pepper and onion, to match picture on page 79.

Chicken in Tomato Towers

2 cups cubed cooked or canned chicken
½ cup diced celery
2 tablespoons chopped pimiento
1 tablespoon chopped onion
¼ teaspoon salt
½ cup mayonnaise
½ to 1 teaspoon curry powder
1 teaspoon lemon juice
6 medium tomatoes

Combine chicken, celery, pimiento, onion, and salt. Blend mayonnaise, curry powder, and lemon juice; add to chicken mixture. Chill.

Peel tomatoes and cut crosswise in 3 slices; sprinkle with salt. On lettuce, reassemble each tomato, top down, spooning filling between slices as you stack. Makes 6 servings.

Salmon-stuffed Tomatoes

1 1-pound can (2 cups) salmon
1 cup pared diced cucumber
1 tablespoon chopped onion
Dash pepper
1 teaspoon salt
1 tablespoon chopped pimiento
1 cup mayonnaise
6 medium tomatoes, chilled

Break salmon in small chunks, removing bones and skin. Combine salmon with cucumber, onion, seasonings, pimiento, and mayonnaise. Chill. Scoop out centers of tomatoes to make cups.

Fill with salmon mixture. Serve on lettuce. Trim with cucumber slices. Makes 6 servings.

Crab-meat Tomato Accordions

1 6½-ounce can (1 cup) crab meat, flaked
½ cup chopped celery
¼ cup chopped green pepper
¼ teaspoon salt
Dash pepper
3 tablespoons lemon juice
⅓ cup mayonnaise
6 medium tomatoes

Combine crab meat, celery, green pepper, salt and pepper. Stir in lemon juice and mayonnaise. Chill. Turn tomatoes stem ends down. Make 5 or 6 downward slices, without cutting to bottom. Fill between slices with crab-meat salad. Place on greens. Pass mayonnaise. Makes 6 servings.

Slice plump juicy garden tomatoes for towers or accordions, or scoop out centers— then spoon in one of these tasty fillings

Tomato Towers march two-by-two down tray trimmed with garden onions, carrot curls, snowy caulifllowerets, and cucumber wedges with bright paprika ridges.

Ripe olives on toothpicks peg tomatoes. Luscious filling is chicken salad.

Egg Salad in Tomato Accordions

6 hard-cooked eggs, chopped
½ cup finely chopped celery
⅓ cup diced green pepper
⅓ cup thinly sliced green onions
2 to 3 tablespoons prepared mustard
½ teaspoon salt
Dash pepper
¼ cup salad dressing or mayonnaise
6 medium tomatoes

Combine eggs, celery, green pepper, onions, mustard, salt, and pepper. Add salad dressing; mix. Chill. Turn tomatoes stem end down. *Without cutting to bottom*, cut down, making 6 slices. Sprinkle cut surfaces with salt. Fill between slices with egg salad. Arrange on crisp salad greens. Garnish with parsley. Makes 6 servings.

Tuna Tomato Stars

1 6½- or 7-ounce can (1 cup) tuna
1 tablespoon lemon juice
2 hard-cooked eggs, chopped
¼ cup thinly sliced sweet pickle
¼ cup finely chopped onion
2 tablespoons diced pimiento
¼ teaspoon salt
Dash pepper
⅓ cup mayonnaise or salad dressing
4 medium tomatoes

Break tuna in chunks and sprinkle with lemon juice; combine with remaining ingredients except tomatoes; mix gently. Chill.

Turn tomatoes stem end down; cut each one *not quite through* in 6 equal sections; spread apart. Sprinkle with salt, fill with tuna salad. Top with carrot curl. Serves 4.

Guacamole, California-style

2 large avocados
1 large tomato
½ small onion, chopped fine
1 tablespoon wine vinegar
Salt and pepper

Peel and chop avocados. Peel and chop tomato, removing the seeds; drain. Put avocado and tomato in blender or mixer bowl; add onion and vinegar. Blend or beat till smooth. Season with salt and pepper to taste. Makes about 1½ cups. Serve in hollowed-out tomato cups as relish, spread.

Tangy Tomatoes

Peel small red-ripe tomatoes. Drizzle them with French dressing and sprinkle with chopped parsley and chives. Chill till serving time. Serve on greens, on salad tray.

Hot Potato Salad in Frankfurter Ring

6 to 8 slices bacon, chopped
¼ cup chopped onion
1 tablespoon enriched flour
1 tablespoon sugar
1½ teaspoons salt
Dash pepper
⅓ cup vinegar
¼ cup water
3 tablespoons salad dressing
4 cups sliced or diced cooked potatoes (4 medium)
¾ teaspoon salt
1 pound (8 to 10) frankfurters, cut in half crosswise
2 hard-cooked eggs, sliced
1 tablespoon minced parsley
½ teaspoon celery seed

Cook bacon till crisp; add onion and cook till tender but not brown. Blend in flour, sugar, 1½ teaspoons salt, and pepper.

Add vinegar and water; cook, stirring constantly, till thick. Remove from heat and stir in salad dressing. Sprinkle potatoes with salt, pour dressing over, and toss lightly.

Stand frankfurter halves upright around inside edge of 8x2-inch round baking dish; fill center with potato salad. (To hold frankfurters in place, put part of salad in center first.) Bake in moderate oven (350°) 20 minutes, or till thoroughly heated. Top with egg slices; sprinkle with parsley and celery seed. Serve hot. Makes 6 to 7 servings.

Skillet Ham-Potato Salad

¼ cup chopped green onions
¼ cup chopped green pepper
1 12-ounce can chopped ham, diced
1 tablespoon fat

• • •

3 cups cooked cubed potatoes
¼ teaspoon salt
Dash pepper
¼ cup mayonnaise or salad dressing

• • •

½ pound sharp process American cheese, diced (1½ cups)

• • •

2 tablespoons chopped parsley

Cook onions, green pepper, and meat in hot fat, stirring occasionally, till meat is lightly browned. Add potatoes, salt, pepper, and mayonnaise. Heat, mixing lightly. Stir in cheese; heat just till it begins to melt. Sprinkle with parsley. Makes 4 servings.

Potato Salad Cups

6 potatoes, cooked in jackets, cubed (4 cups)
1 onion, chopped
3 hard-cooked eggs, sliced
1 cup chopped celery
1 cucumber, diced
1½ teaspoons salt
¼ teaspoon paprika
¼ cup French dressing

• • •

Mayonnaise or Cooked Dressing
1 teaspoon celery seed

Combine first 7 ingredients; chill in French dressing 4 to 6 hours. Before serving, add just enough mayonnaise to moisten and mix gently. Add celery seed. Pack in custard cups; unmold on lettuce. Makes 8 servings.

Red-n'-green Potato Salad: Add ½ cup sliced radishes and ⅓ cup chopped green pepper to potato mixture. Add 1 cup cubed ham in place of celery seed. Serve in large bowl.

Quick ways to peel tomatoes:

Run back of knife over skin of tomato to loosen it; peel.

Some cooks prefer to plunge tomatoes in boiling water or twirl them over flame to loosen skin. Quick, don't cook!

Picnic? Porch supper? It's potato-salad time!

Perfect Potato Salad

3 cups cubed or sliced cooked potatoes
1 teaspoon sugar
1 teaspoon vinegar
¼ cup chopped onion
½ cup sliced celery (if desired)
¼ cup sliced sweet pickle (if desired)
1½ teaspoons salt
1½ teaspoons celery seed
¾ cup mayonnaise
2 hard-cooked eggs, sliced

Sprinkle potatoes with sugar and vinegar. Add onion, celery, pickle, seasonings, and mayonnaise; toss to blend. Carefully "fold in" egg slices. Chill. Serve in lettuce-lined bowl. Trim with egg slices. Makes 4 servings.

Parsleyed Potato Salad

½ cup minced parsley
¼ cup chopped green pepper
¼ cup minced celery tops
¼ cup chopped green onions
¼ cup chopped dill pickle
8 cups diced cooked potatoes
½ cup sliced celery

• • •

1 cup mayonnaise
¼ cup clear French dressing
2 to 2½ teaspoons salt
½ teaspoon pepper
1 teaspoon dry mustard

Mix ¼ *cup* of the parsley with next four ingredients; take out half of mixture and to it add rest of parsley; set aside. Toss remainder of mixture with potatoes and celery.

Combine mayonnaise, dressing, seasonings; add to salad. Toss. Pack lightly into 8x8x2-inch pan or shallow 2-quart baking dish. Sprinkle reserved parsley mixture on top. Chill. Lift out servings with pancake turner. Makes 9 to 12 servings.

Sour-cream Potato Salad

6 cups diced, cooked potatoes
¼ cup chopped green onions and tops
1 teaspoon celery seed
1½ teaspoons salt
½ teaspoon pepper
4 hard-cooked eggs

• • •

1 cup dairy sour cream
½ cup mayonnaise
¼ cup vinegar
1 teaspoon prepared mustard

• • •

¾ cup diced pared cucumber

Combine potatoes, onions, celery seed, salt, and pepper. Toss lightly. Separate whites of hard-cooked eggs from yolks; chop whites and add to potato mixture. Chill.

Mash hard-cooked yolks; add sour cream, mayonnaise, vinegar, and mustard. Mix well. Pour dressing over potatoes; toss lightly. Let stand 20 minutes. Just before serving, add cucumber. Trim with minced parsley.

Makes 6 servings.

Cook potatoes in boiling salted water, peel and cube—they're salad-ready

1 Scrub potatoes thoroughly with a firm vegetable brush. Choose potatoes of equal size so all will get done at the same time.

2 Cook potatoes in boiling, salted water. Begin fork-testing after 35 minutes of cooking. When just tender, remove from heat and drain. Shake in pan over low heat to dry.

3 Peel potatoes while hot, holding on long fork or on paper towel. Salad secret: Mix salad with warm potatoes—they absorb seasonings.

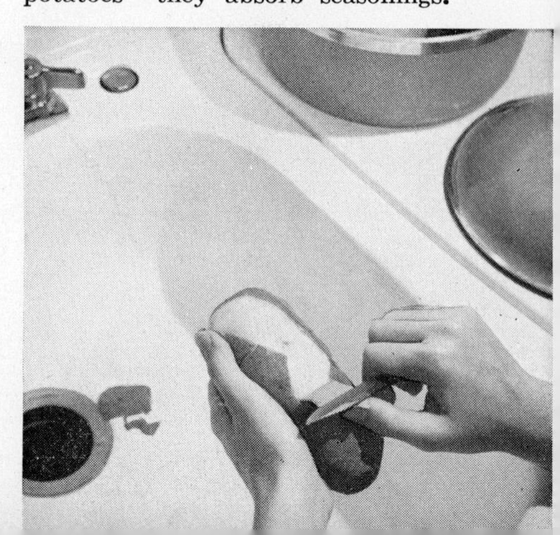

Bill Hopkins; Allen Snook, Inc.

4 Halve potatoes lengthwise. With flat side down on cutting board, slice each potato half in ¾-inch strips. Then cut it crosswise to make bite-size cubes.

Comin' up—potato salad, hot dogs!

It's a perfect 4th—warm, sunny. And the picnic's ready! Pass the mustard, pickle relish—onion, too. Put the iced tray of carrot and celery sticks, rosy radishes where everyone can reach. Pour chilly milk for the youngsters, hot coffee for the grownups. Top off with plump wedges of warm blueberry pie!

We show Perfect Potato Salad, flavor-blended to mellow goodness. Try all our others, too—hot, tangy, herb-flavored. They're all year-round favorites.

Tasty **molded** vegetable salads

They're chock-full of crunchy goodness—the family favorites and company specials alike. And they double nicely as meat accompaniments

Potato-Salad Mold

1 envelope (1 tablespoon) unflavored gelatin
2 tablespoons sugar
1 teaspoon salt
1¼ cups boiling water
¼ cup lemon juice
• • •
8 stuffed green olives, sliced
3 hard-cooked eggs, chopped
4 cups diced cooked potatoes
1 cup diced celery
¼ cup diced green pepper
¼ cup diced pimiento
¼ cup chopped green onions
¼ cup chopped parsley
1½ teaspoons salt
1 cup mayonnaise
½ cup heavy cream, whipped

Mix gelatin, sugar, and salt thoroughly; pour boiling water over and stir to dissolve sugar. Add lemon juice. Pour thin layer of mixture into 1½-quart ring mold; chill.

When gelatin layer is almost firm, place "flower" design on top (olive slices and green-pepper strips).

Add remaining ingredients to rest of gelatin mixture. Spoon over gelatin in ring mold. Chill till firm. Makes 8 servings.

Beet Relish Cups

1 package lemon-flavored gelatin
1¼ cups boiling water
¾ cup beet liquid
2 tablespoons vinegar
½ teaspoon salt
1 teaspoon horseradish
1 teaspoon Worcestershire sauce
1 teaspoon grated onion
4 drops Tabasco sauce
• • •
1½ cups canned diced beets, drained
½ cup diced celery

Dissolve gelatin in boiling water. Add next 7 ingredients. Chill mixture till partially set. Fold in diced beets and celery. Turn into individual molds, chill till firm. Makes about 12 servings.

← *Have a Dutch lunch treat*

Help yourself to Potato-salad Mold, tomato slices on lettuce, salami cornucopias. Stack up ham, cheese, and plenty of mustard on a slice of rye. Cup of coffee makes it a meal.

Cool-as-a-cucumber Salads

1 package lime-flavored gelatin
¾ cup boiling water
¼ cup lemon juice
1 teaspoon onion juice
1 cup dairy sour cream
1 cup chopped unpared cucumber

Dissolve gelatin in boiling water. Add lemon and onion juices. Chill till partially set. Stir in sour cream and cucumber.

Pour into 6 individual molds and chill till firm. Unmold. (See picture, page 79.)

Cucumber Ring

Cucumber-trim layer: (Optional)

½ envelope (1½ teaspoons) unflavored gelatin
1 tablespoon sugar
½ teaspoon salt
¾ cup boiling water
2 tablespoons lemon juice
Thin slices unpared cucumber

Thoroughly mix gelatin, sugar, and salt. Pour boiling water over and stir to dissolve sugar. Add lemon juice.

Overlap cucumber slices in bottom of 6½-cup ring mold (see page 144). Pour gelatin mixture carefully over them. Chill firm.

Cucumber-salad layer:

1 envelope (1 tablespoon) unflavored gelatin
2 tablespoons sugar
¾ teaspoon salt
⅔ cup boiling water
3 to 4 tablespoons lemon juice
About 6 medium cucumbers, pared
1 8-ounce package cream cheese
1 cup mayonnaise or salad dressing
¼ cup minced onion
¼ cup minced parsley

Thoroughly mix gelatin, sugar, and salt. Pour boiling water over and stir to dissolve sugar. Add lemon juice.

Halve cucumbers, scrape out seeds; put through food chopper, using fine blade. (Measure 2 cups drained ground cucumber.)

Soften cream cheese; add cucumber, mayonnaise, onion, and parsley, mixing well. Stir in gelatin mixture. Pour over firm gelatin in mold (or mold without trim layer).

Unmold on greens. Makes 8 servings.

Cabbage, radishes add crunch to gelatin

Perfection Salad

2 envelopes (2 tablespoons) unflavored gelatin
½ cup sugar
1 teaspoon salt
2½ cups boiling water
½ cup vinegar
2 tablespoons lemon juice, fresh, frozen, or canned
1½ cups *very* finely shredded cabbage
1 cup chopped celery
¼ cup chopped pimiento
½ cup chopped green pepper

Thoroughly mix gelatin, sugar, salt; add boiling water, stirring till sugar dissolves. Add vinegar and lemon juice. Cool. When mixture begins to thicken, add remaining ingredients. Pour into 8½x4½x2½-inch loaf pan, or 10 individual molds. Chill firm.

Unmold on lettuce. Garnish with ripe olive halves. Loaf makes 8 to 10 servings.

When you're entertaining the crowd, make a double recipe in twin loaves, as shown in picture below.

Coleslaw Parfait Salad

1 package lemon-flavored gelatin
1 cup boiling water
½ cup mayonnaise
½ cup cold water
2 tablespoons vinegar
¼ teaspoon salt

• • •

1½ cups *finely* shredded cabbage
½ cup radish slices
½ cup diced celery
2 to 4 tablespoons diced green pepper
1 tablespoon diced onion

Dissolve gelatin in boiling water. Blend in mayonnaise, cold water, vinegar, and salt.

Chill mixture until partially set. Then beat till fluffy. Add cabbage, radish slices, celery, green pepper, and onion.

Pour into individual molds or 1-quart mold; chill till set.

To match picture, unmold on ruffles of lettuce and garnish salads with thin slices of radish and leaves of mint.

Makes 6 to 8 servings.

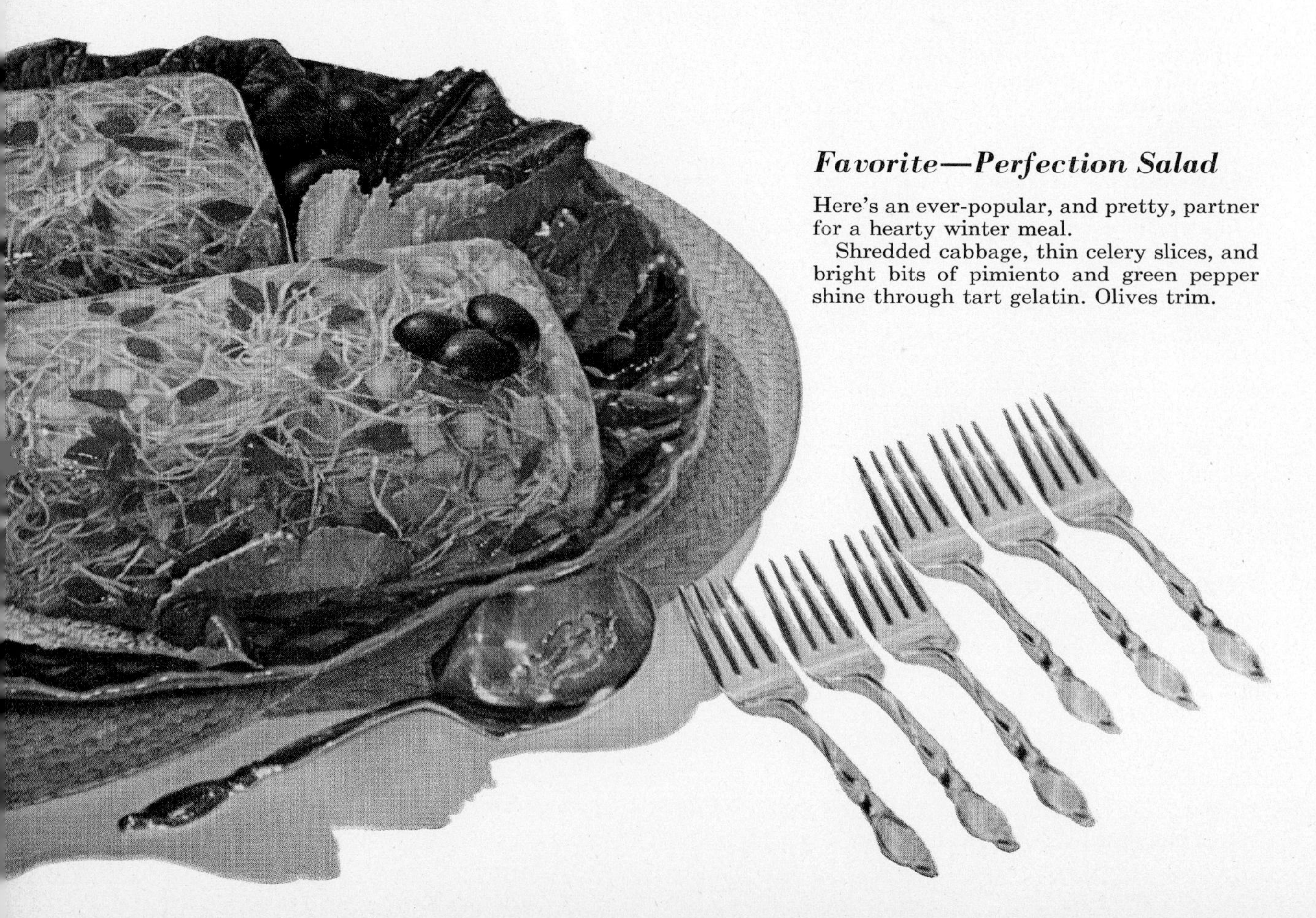

Favorite—Perfection Salad

Here's an ever-popular, and pretty, partner for a hearty winter meal.

Shredded cabbage, thin celery slices, and bright bits of pimiento and green pepper shine through tart gelatin. Olives trim.

Coleslaw Parfait Salad—refreshing, smooth!

This fluffy molded salad has a tangy dressing built right in. Whipped lemony gelatin mixture is chock-full of crisp shredded cabbage, celery. Thin radish slices and bits of green pepper add sparkle; diced onion gives snap. This year-round salad has a freshness especially nice in winter.

Vegetables in Jellied Bouillon

2 envelopes (2 tablespoons) unflavored gelatin
2 cups canned condensed bouillon or consomme
1½ tablespoons vinegar
Salt to taste
Paprika
1 cup finely shredded cabbage
¼ cup diced celery
¼ cup chopped green pepper

Soften gelatin in ½ cup of the cold bouillon. Dissolve over boiling water. Remove from heat and add remaining bouillon, vinegar, salt, and paprika.

Chill until partially set. Fold in vegetables. Pour into individual molds. Chill till firm. Makes 4 servings.

Calico Vegetable Molds

1 package lemon-flavored gelatin
1¾ cups boiling water
2 tablespoons vinegar
¼ teaspoon salt

• • •

½ cup cooked drained sliced or diced carrots
½ cup cooked or canned drained peas
¼ cup radish slices
3 tablespoons green-onion slices

Dissolve gelatin in boiling water; add vinegar and salt. Chill till partially set.

Add vegetables. Pour into individual molds. Chill till set. Unmold on salad greens. Trim with radish roses, if desired. Pass bowl of mayonnaise or salad dressing.

Makes 4 to 6 servings.

Make salads or main dishes

Fill aspic ring with seafood salad to make main dish. Serve individual aspics with meat

For summer—salad supper

Circle ring of Old-time Tomato Aspic with thick ham slices, deviled eggs, your favorite rolls. Wreath center bowl of mayonnaise with curly endive. Pass iced tea or fruit punch, and cantaloupe a la mode.

# of these tangy well-seasoned tomato aspics

Easy Aspic

2 packages lemon-flavored gelatin
2½ cups boiling water
2 8-ounce cans (2 cups) seasoned tomato sauce
2 tablespoons vinegar
½ teaspoon salt
½ teaspoon seasoned salt

Dissolve gelatin in boiling water; add tomato sauce, vinegar, and seasonings. Pour into 6-cup mold or individual molds. Chill till firm. Unmold on crisp greens.

Makes 8 servings.

Old-time Tomato Aspic

4 cups tomato juice
⅓ cup chopped onion
¼ cup chopped celery leaves
2 tablespoons brown sugar
1 teaspoon salt
2 small bay leaves
4 whole cloves
2 envelopes (2 tablespoons) unflavored gelatin
¼ cup cold water
3 tablespoons lemon juice
1 cup finely diced celery

Combine tomato juice, onion, celery leaves, brown sugar, salt, bay leaves, and cloves. Simmer 5 minutes. Strain. Soften gelatin in cold water; dissolve in the hot tomato mixture. Add lemon juice. Chill till partially set. Add celery. Pour into 5- or 6-cup ring mold. Chill till set. Serve with chicken salad, if desired. Makes 8 to 10 servings.

Cheesed Tomato Aspic

2½ cups tomato juice
2 bay leaves
4 peppercorns
½ teaspoon onion salt
½ teaspoon celery salt
½ teaspoon oregano
½ teaspoon salt
Dash pepper
2 envelopes (2 tablespoons) unflavored gelatin

• • •

2 3-ounce packages cream cheese
1½ cups tomato juice

• • •

1 6-ounce can (⅔ cup) evaporated milk, whipped

Blend *2 cups* tomato juice and seasonings. Simmer 5 minutes; strain. Soften gelatin in remaining ½ cup tomato juice; dissolve in hot mixture. Cool to lukewarm.

Soften cheese; blend in 1½ cups cold tomato juice. Combine two mixtures. Chill till partially set. Fold in whipped milk. Pour into 5½-cup mold; chill firm. Serve with crisp relishes. Makes 10 to 12 servings.

Peter Piper had nothing on us — here's a relish line-up that will suit any pickle fan! In center is tart, tangy Piccalilli Mold — special treat when it's paired with roast pork, veal, or beef. Stuffed-pickle Slices (see how-to, page 143) line up atop. Dishes hold candied dill sticks, pickled onions, pickle slices and mustard pickles.

Fresh flavor of lemony orange gelatin, crunch of garden vegetables, tang of sweet pickle — *that's* what Carrot-'n-Cabbage Tower is made of. Here, plump pear halves make a pretty trim.

Pair vegetables, fruit flavors in winter sparklers

All-occasion favorite—Sunshine Salad

Give traditional pineapple-carrot salad a perk-up trim — pineapple-tidbit flower has walnut center, green-pepper stem and leaves.

Carrot-'n-Cabbage Tower

2 packages orange-flavored gelatin
2 cups boiling water
1½ cups orange juice
¼ cup lemon juice, fresh, frozen, or canned
¼ teaspoon salt

• • •

1 cup shredded cabbage
⅔ cup grated carrot
½ cup diced celery
6 tablespoons diced sweet pickle, or sweet pickle relish

• • •

Chilled pared fresh or canned pear halves
Lemon juice, if using fresh pears

Dissolve gelatin in boiling water; add fruit juices and salt. Chill till partially set. Add vegetables and pickle. Pour into tall 1½-quart mold or individual molds. Chill till set. Unmold on leaf lettuce, if desired.

Core fresh pear halves, or drain canned ones. Dip fresh pears in lemon juice to keep them bright. Arrange around mold, as shown in picture. Makes 8 to 10 servings.

Harvest Vegetable Loaf

2 packages lemon-flavored gelatin
3½ cups boiling water
3 tablespoons vinegar
½ teaspoon salt

• • •

9 to 12 long green beans, cooked
3 or 4 long strips pimiento

• • •

1 cup cooked cauliflowerets
½ cup cooked sliced carrots
¼ cup diced celery
¼ cup sliced radishes
¼ cup sliced green onions

Dissolve gelatin in boiling water; add vinegar and salt. Pour about ½ inch of gelatin mixture into 8½x4½x2½-inch loaf pan. Chill until set. Divide beans in 3 or 4 bundles and circle each with pimiento strip. Arrange on gelatin in pan.

Chill remaining gelatin till partially set; pour enough over beans to cover; chill until firm.

Meanwhile combine remaining gelatin with rest of vegetables (but do not chill). Pour over firm gelatin in pan, then chill till set. Unmold on greens. Makes 8 servings.

Sunshine Salad

1 package lemon-flavored gelatin
1 cup boiling water
1 No. 2 can (2½ cups) crushed pineapple
1 tablespoon vinegar
½ teaspoon salt
1 cup grated carrot
⅓ cup chopped pecans

Dissolve gelatin in boiling water. Drain pineapple, reserving syrup. Add water to syrup to make 1 cup; add to gelatin, with vinegar and salt. Chill till partially set.

Fold carrot, pineapple, and nuts into gelatin. Turn into individual molds or 10x6x1½-inch pan. Chill till firm. Unmold on greens.

Makes 6 servings.

(To match picture, double the recipe and mold in 9½x5x3-inch loaf pan.)

Piccalilli Mold

1 package lime- or lemon-flavored gelatin
2 cups boiling water
Dash salt
2 tablespoons vinegar from pickled onions
3 tablespoons thinly sliced pickled onions
½ cup sweet piccalilli

Dissolve gelatin in boiling water. Add salt and vinegar. Chill till partially set.

Fold in remaining ingredients; turn into small individual molds or shallow pan. (To match picture, use 6½x4x2½-inch refrigerator dish.) Chill firm. Serves 7 to 8.

Summer Garden Molds

1 package lemon-flavored gelatin
1½ cups boiling water
1 teaspoon salt
3 tablespoons lemon juice
2 tablespoons vinegar
1 cup diced celery
½ cup diced cucumber
¼ cup green-pepper strips
2 tablespoons diced carrot
1 tablespoon chopped green onion

Dissolve gelatin in boiling water; add salt, lemon juice, and vinegar. Chill till partially set. Stir in vegetables. Pour into individual molds or 1-quart mold; chill till firm. Unmold on lettuce. Makes 6 to 8 servings.

Meat, poultry, and seafood salads

These are salads that are *unusual*-ly delicious, have a special flair. (Some, like the Green Goddess, are chef-famous.) Some are extra easy, some take a little more doing—and a little more daring. So what might you be looking for?

. . . an *appetizer* for a special family or company dinner? How-to pictures will tell you exactly how to prepare shrimp; recipes give you the wonderful sauces we've found the best. Look, too, for crab, lobster, oyster, beef, and ham specialities.

. . . a *seafood salad* for a hot-day luncheon? There's a basic recipe you'll want to rely on. Then see all the tips to give a new twist to the serving. Don't feel stumped on the what-to-eat-with. The ideas are there.

. . . a *hearty salad bowl*—a chef salad, a Caesar salad? Meal-in-a-bowl, we call them. They make a fine summer supper, go over so big with men they'll often do the concocting.

. . . a really elegant *chicken or turkey salad*? You'll find that, too, *and* the way to stew a chicken specially for salad, so it will be most flavorful.

. . . a cool *molded salad*, something on the spectacular side, you hope? There are beautiful double-deckers on pages 114, 115; one's the eyecatcher on a tray of smorgasbord relishes.

. . . pretty-as-the-picture arrangements for *salad plates and platters*? Turn the page to find these. Real cool masterpieces.

Have a salad meal on a sizzler of a day

← Chicken Buffet Molds (page 110) are perfect for a porch supper. Serve with sticks, slices, and rounds of cheese, roll-ups of ham and cold cuts, golden deviled eggs, and little green onions, carrot curls, radish roses. Roll a cool butter ball for each hot, sugary blueberry muffin; pass tall glasses of tinkling pink lemonade.

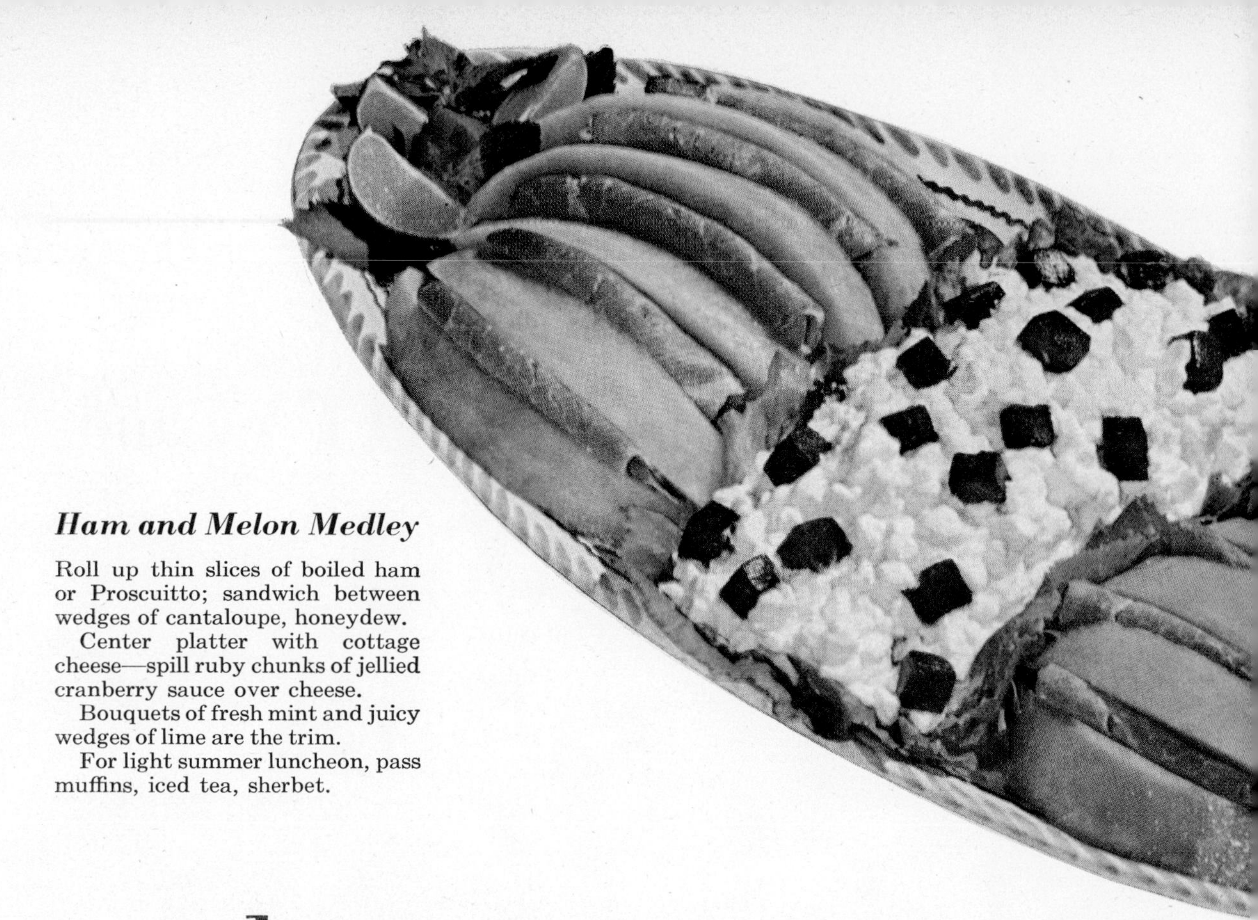

Ham and Melon Medley

Roll up thin slices of boiled ham or Proscuitto; sandwich between wedges of cantaloupe, honeydew.

Center platter with cottage cheese—spill ruby chunks of jellied cranberry sauce over cheese.

Bouquets of fresh mint and juicy wedges of lime are the trim.

For light summer luncheon, pass muffins, iced tea, sherbet.

Fill platters with meat salads, fruit;

Ham-'n-Eggs, Salad-style, with fruit

Ham's wrapped around fruit surprise, in Banana-Ham Rolls; eggs are deviled. Platter partners are thin melon slices, pineapple chunks, and ripe strawberry halves.

Shrimp Salad Plate

For shore supper at home, how about shrimp salad trimmed with egg chunks, lemon, ripe olives?

Go-withs —pear half with blueberries, melon balls, tomato-cucumber accordions, green onions.

pass bread, beverage—it's a meal!

Banana Ham Rolls

6 thin slices boiled ham
Prepared mustard
3 medium green-tipped bananas, peeled
Melted butter or margarine

Spread ham slices lightly with mustard. Cut bananas in half crosswise; wrap ham slice around each half; fasten with toothpick. Place on greased shallow baking pan; brush with butter. Bake in moderate oven (350°) about 25 minutes, or till bananas are tender. Serve hot. Makes 6 servings.

Meat Salad Platter and Plate Suggestions:

Serve individual molds of Jellied Chicken Almond (page 111) with crisp cucumber sticks, ripe olives, tomato flowers, tangy pickles, and frosted grapes. (See page 143.)

Fill avocado halves with chicken or seafood salad. Team up with orange sections and pineapple rings topped with raspberries (see picture, page 21). Round out meal with hot rolls, cold milk, and munchy cookies.

Shrimp Tower

Pink shrimp (split in half) are to dip in chili sauce in green-pepper cup. They're crowning touch on stack-up of avocado, tomato slices, fluffy Boston lettuce.

Cartwheels of tomato and lemon, triangles of Cheddar cheese ring salad.

Go glamorous with meat and seafood appetizers

Choose shrimp with hot sauce or beef in tangy sour cream

Shrimp Cocktail With Chili Hot Sauce

¾ cup chili sauce
¼ cup lemon juice
1 to 2 tablespoons prepared horseradish
1 teaspoon minced onion
2 teaspoons Worcestershire sauce
4 drops Tabasco sauce
Dash salt
Fresh-cooked Shrimp

Combine ingredients except shrimp. Chill thoroughly. Makes 1 cup Hot Sauce.

Serve in individual cocktail cups as shown above. Hook shrimp over rims of glasses. For trim, snip pointed fans from romaine.

Sour Cream-Tarragon Dip

1 cup dairy sour cream
⅔ cup mayonnaise or salad dressing
1 teaspoon vinegar
¼ teaspoon monosodium glutamate
¼ teaspoon seasoned salt
½ teaspoon tarragon or few leaves fresh tarragon

Combine ingredients and chill. Serve with seafood as an appetizer. Makes 1⅔ cups.

Speedy Shrimp Dip

Blend ½ cup mayonnaise and ¼ cup spicy meat sauce. Serve with shrimp.

Prepare Fresh-cooked Shrimp this way

1 Add spicy flavor to shrimp while they cook. For 4 pounds of fresh or frozen shrimp in shells, measure 9 cups water into kettle. Add ¼ cup salt, ¼ cup vinegar, 3 bay leaves, 2 teaspoons pickling or shrimp spice, and 2 stalks celery. Bring water to boiling; add shrimp.

Corral shrimp in fry basket

2 We show shrimp cooked in shells, but you may shell and devein them first if you wish — cooking spice has a better chance to penetrate and back edges ruffle prettily. (If cooked in basket, they're easy to lift out.)

Shrimp Remoulade

⅓ cup olive oil or salad oil
1 teaspoon salt
½ teaspoon pepper
1 teaspoon horse-radish
2 tablespoons vinegar
4 teaspoons Creole mustard or other hot-type mustard
¼ cup finely chopped onion
1 cup finely chopped celery hearts
1 tablespoon chopped parsley

• • •

1½ cups shredded lettuce
2 pounds cooked cleaned shrimp

Combine all ingredients except lettuce and shrimp. Chill. Makes 1⅓ cups Remoulade Sauce.

Just before serving, arrange shredded lettuce on individual salad plates or on shells. Place shrimp atop. Pour Remoulade Sauce over. Trim with sprigs of parsley.

Makes about 6 appetizer-servings.

Herbed Seafood Sauce

¼ cup finely chopped sweet pickle
2½ tablespoons finely chopped green onion
1 tablespoon minced parsley
½ clove garlic, minced

• • •

2 cups mayonnaise
1 teaspoon dry mustard
1 teaspoon paprika
½ teaspoon salt
Dash pepper

Mix pickle, onion, parsley, and garlic. Put in fine sieve; press to extract as much juice as possible. Add juice to mayonnaise. Stir in remaining ingredients. Serve as sauce or dip with seafood. Makes 2 cups.

Pickled Shrimp with Onion

2½ pounds fresh or frozen shrimp
½ cup celery tops
¼ cup mixed pickling spice
3½ teaspoons salt

• • •

2 cups sliced onion
7 to 8 bay leaves

• • •

1¼ cups salad oil
¾ cup white vinegar
3 tablespoons capers and juice
2½ teaspoons celery seed
1½ teaspoons salt
6 or 7 drops Tabasco sauce

Cover shrimp with boiling water; add celery tops, spices, and salt. Cook as shown below. Drain, peel, and devein.

Alternate cleaned shrimp and onion in shallow bowl. Add bay leaves.

Combine remaining ingredients and pour over shrimp. Chill at least 24 hours. (Pickled shrimp will keep at least a week in the refrigerator.) Drain; remove bay leaves.

Serve shrimp and onion slices on relish tray or in tiny individual dishes. Makes 6 to 8 appetizer-servings.

Pickled Shrimp-Egg Salad: Omit onion and celery seed in above recipe. Add 1 cup celery slices, ½ cup chopped onion, and ½ cup diced green pepper to pickling marinade.

Pour over shrimp and chill 24 hours. Drain shrimp, reserving marinade; remove bay leaves. Slice 3 hard-cooked eggs, add to shrimp and toss lightly.

Serve on lettuce with the marinade or mayonnaise. If desired, garnish with extra hard-cooked egg. Makes about 6 servings.

Time carefully—don't overcook

3 When water returns to boil, set timer for 5 minutes. Cover pan, reduce heat, simmer gently. Remove from heat soon as timer-bell rings. (Uncooked shrimp is usually gray-green; it changes to pink or red when cooked.)

Last—drain, peel if necessary

4 If shrimp are cooked in shells, rinse in cool water to make peeling job easier. Split shell on underneath side; peel back from opening (shell uncooked shrimp same way). Remove dark vein along back of shrimp with tip of knife. Chill. Serve with sauce or dip. Makes 12 servings.

Grapefruit-Crab Cocktail

1 6½-ounce can (1 cup) crab meat, chilled and drained
Lemon juice
1 1-pound can (2 cups) grapefruit segments, chilled and drained
1 cup mayonnaise or salad dressing
2 tablespoons catsup
1 tablespoon lemon juice
Few drops Tabasco sauce

Flake crab meat, removing bony bits. Sprinkle with lemon juice.

Alternate grapefruit and crab meat in cocktail glasses. Combine remaining ingredients to make sauce; pour over. Serves 6 to 8.

Oysters on the Half Shell

Each guest rates a plate of tiny oysters on shells, atop a chilly bed of crushed ice. Trim with fluffs of parsley or water cress and a tart lemon wedge. Pass Tabasco sauce.

Serve individual cups of Chili Hot Sauce (see recipe with Shrimp Cocktail, page 98) for dipping.

Oysters are easier to prepare if you have the shells opened at the market. Allow 6 small oysters for each guest.

Toss away flat upper shell. With knife, loosen oyster from deep half shell. Remove shell bits. Chill. Serve on deep half shell.

(If oysters in shells are not available, serve shucked oysters in lettuce-lined cocktail glasses with the sauce spooned over.

For 6 servings, allow 1 pint fresh oysters or two 12-ounce cans frozen raw oysters.)

Lobster-ettes

Nestle steaming-hot miniature red lobster tails (in shells) beside water cress. Offer lemon wedges, drawn butter, cocktail and tartare sauces. Fork bites out of shell and dip!

For this appetizer plate, buy dainty frozen 1- to 2-ounce lobster tails (they come from Denmark). Thaw, then butterfly this way: With sharp knife, cut lengthwise along back, but not through undershell. Spread open in butterfly fashion; remove sand vein. Brush meat with melted butter or margarine.

Place shell down on broiler-pan rack. Broil 3 inches from heat about 7 minutes or till done, brushing frequently with melted butter. Sprinkle with paprika and serve immediately. (Or, cook shrimp-style, page 98.)

Cold, Marinated Beef Slices are an appetizer-specialty at Chicago's Stock Yard Inn. Tangy sour cream, lemon juice, accent beef flavor. Trim is green pepper, pimiento, ripe olive.

Cold, Marinated Beef Slices

½ pound cooked sirloin steak *or* beef roast, cut in thin strips
1 small onion, thinly sliced and separated in rings
¾ teaspoon salt
Dash pepper
1½ tablespoons lemon juice
1 cup dairy sour cream

Combine beef strips, onion rings, salt, and pepper. Sprinkle lemon juice over meat mixture and mix in sour cream. Chill. Serve in lettuce-lined dishes. Makes 6 servings.

Ham-Chutney Roll-ups

Spread thin ham slices lightly with butter and finely chopped chutney. Roll up, beginning with narrow side. Chill. Slice on "bias."

Golden Liverwurst Balls

Blend 1 cup liverwurst and 2 teaspoons finely chopped onion. Form in 1-inch balls; roll in ½ cup grated carrot. Cover and chill.

Try **main dish** salads in summer

Crunchy Baked Ham Salad

3 cups diced, cooked ham
1 cup diced celery
½ cup chopped stuffed green olives
2 hard-cooked eggs, diced
¼ cup chopped onion
1 tablespoon lemon juice, fresh, frozen, or canned
1 tablespoon prepared mustard
Dash pepper
¾ cup mayonnaise or salad dressing
1 cup crushed potato chips

Combine all ingredients except the potato chips. Place in an 8x2-inch round baking dish. Sprinkle with the crushed potato chips. Bake in a hot oven (400°) 20 to 25 minutes. Makes 6 servings.

Ham Salad

1½ cups diced cooked or canned ham
6 hard-cooked eggs, coarsely diced
½ cup diced celery
½ cup sliced gherkins

• • •

⅓ cup mayonnaise or salad dressing
2 tablespoons prepared mustard
1 tablespoon lemon juice, fresh, frozen, or canned

• • •

Salt and pepper

Combine ham, eggs, celery, and gherkins. Blend mayonnaise, mustard, and lemon juice; add to ham mixture, and toss lightly. Season to taste with salt and pepper. Chill.
Makes 6 servings.

Bacon-topped Chef's Bowl

1 head lettuce
1 12-ounce can luncheon meat, cut in strips
½ cup sliced celery
6 strips crisp bacon, crumbled
2 hard-cooked eggs, sliced
1 teaspoon salt
French dressing

Break cold, crisp lettuce into salad bowl. Add remaining ingredients and toss lightly.
Makes 6 servings.

Salami-Swiss Cheese Salad

1 head lettuce
¼ pound salami, cubed
¼ pound Swiss cheese, cut in strips
½ cup sliced ripe olives
1 4-ounce can (½ cup) pimiento, chopped
2 tomatoes, cut in eighths
1 2-ounce can (3 tablespoons) anchovies, chopped

• • •

⅓ cup salad oil
3 tablespoons wine vinegar
½ teaspoon salt
Dash pepper
1 clove garlic, minced

Break lettuce in bite-size chunks. Add salami, cheese, olives, pimiento, tomatoes, and anchovies.

In jar, combine oil, vinegar, salt, pepper, and garlic for dressing. Shake well. Pour dressing over vegetables and toss lightly.

Makes 8 to 10 servings.

Bill Hopkins

tips

For salad use, cut loaf-style meat and cheese in thin strips: Using French knife, cut meat in ½-inch lengthwise slices; stack and cut in ½-inch wide strips. Cut cheese with cheese slicer, making thinner strips.

Chef's and Caesar salads rate tops with men

Chef's Bowl

1 clove garlic
1 head romaine or lettuce
1 to 2 cups cooked or canned ham, in strips
½ pound American cheese, in strips
1½ pounds fresh asparagus, cooked, drained, and chilled
2 cups cooked peas, chilled
1 bunch radishes
Deviled Eggs (page 118)

Rub salad bowl with cut clove of garlic. Line it with romaine. Arrange ham and cheese, vegetables, and Deviled Eggs as shown. Sprinkle with salt and freshly ground pepper.

Serve salad, then pass Chef's French Dressing. Makes 6 servings.

Chef's French Dressing: Combine 2 tablespoons sugar, 1 teaspoon salt, 1 teaspoon dry mustard, 1 teaspoon paprika. Add ⅓ cup herb vinegar, 3 tablespoons lemon juice, 1 tablespoon grated onion, and ⅔ cup salad oil. Cover and shake. Makes 1⅓ cups.

Caesar Salad

Prepare garlic olive oil one to several days early: Slice 6 cloves garlic lengthwise in quarters and let stand in 1 cup oil.

Caesar Croutons: Cut each slice bread in 5 strips each way—make 1 cup squares. Spread on cooky sheet; pour a little garlic oil over. Heat in oven at 225° 2 hours. Sprinkle with Parmesan cheese. Refrigerate in jar.

Wash 3 medium heads romaine lettuce 24 hours ahead. Pat dry; wrap in towels; chill.

At *last minute*, break romaine leaves in 2- or 3-inch widths into chilled salad bowl. Drizzle ⅓ cup garlic oil over greens, then 2 or 3 tablespoons wine vinegar. Squeeze 1 lemon over, using fork to help free juice.

Break in one or two 1-minute coddled eggs. Grind pepper over all. Season with salt and dash of Worcestershire sauce. Sprinkle with 6 tablespoons grated Parmesan cheese.

Roll-toss 6 or 7 times. Add croutons; toss once; serve on chilled plates. Trim with rolled anchovies. Makes main course for 6.

Ham-Chicken Bowl Supreme

1 clove garlic
1 head lettuce

• • •

1 cup diced cucumber
1 green pepper, cut in narrow strips
1 cup cooked or canned ham, cut in strips
1 cup cooked or canned chicken, cut in strips
3 hard-cooked eggs, sliced
2 tomatoes, cut in wedges

• • •

½ cup salad oil
3 tablespoons vinegar
1 tablespoon prepared horseradish
½ teaspoon Worcestershire sauce
2 drops Tabasco sauce
½ teaspoon salt
⅛ teaspoon pepper

Rub salad bowl with cut clove of garlic. Break lettuce into bite-size pieces in bowl.

Arrange cucumber, green pepper, ham, chicken, eggs, and tomatoes atop.

Combine remaining ingredients to make the dressing. Cover and shake thoroughly. Serve salad and pass dressing.

Makes 8 to 10 servings.

Ham and Turkey Toss

1 small head lettuce
2 heads Bibb lettuce
½ bunch curly endive or romaine

• • •

2 cups narrow strips of ham
1½ cups narrow strips of turkey
2 slices Swiss cheese, cut in strips
1 avocado, sliced
1 2-ounce can anchovy fillets

• • •

Italian dressing

Break up greens into wooden bowl. On greens, arrange remaining ingredients, except dressing. Top salad with hard-cooked egg slices, olives, and pickles, if desired.

Pour dressing over and toss at table. Pass additional dressing. Makes 8 servings.

Each of these hearty salads is a meal-in-a-bowl; best way we know to finish up that holiday ham or turkey—with company!

Here's spring supper in your salad bowl. With Chef's Bowl, pass mugs of hot tomato bouillon, crisp Garlic Rounds, hot rolls. Dessert is banana cream pie, coffee.

Try seafood fix-ups with a salt-air tang!

Basic Seafood Salad

1 5- or 6½-ounce can tuna, crab, lobster, or shrimp, or 1 cup any seafood
1 to 2 tablespoons lemon juice
1 cup sliced celery
¼ cup salad dressing or mayonnaise
Salt and pepper to taste

Break seafood in chunks or flake it, if necessary. Sprinkle with lemon juice. Add celery and salad dressing. Mix lightly; season. Chill. Serve with lemon wedges. Serves 4.

Crab Salad with Cucumber: Follow directions for Crab Salad in Basic recipe, above. Add ¼ cup diced unpared cucumber just before serving. Top with egg slices, capers.

Shrimp Salad in Avocado Cups: Follow directions for Shrimp Salad in Basic recipe, left. Cut up shrimp. Add 2 tablespoons chopped green onion and, just before serving, ¼ cup diced unpared cucumber. Mound in four lemon-juice-brushed avocado halves.

Lobster in Seashell: Follow directions for Lobster Salad in Basic recipe, left. Heap each serving in lettuce-lined seashell. Top with thin avocado slices. (At Neiman-Marcus in Dallas, mother-of-pearl shells are used, as shown. Halve oranges with zigzag cut and sprinkle with minced parsley, for trim.)

Shrimp With Lime Rings

1 package lime-flavored gelatin
1¾ cups boiling water
3 tablespoons lemon juice
¼ teaspoon salt
1 12-ounce carton (1½ cups) large-curd cream-style cottage cheese, drained
Mayonnaise
Capers
Cooked or canned cleaned shrimp

Dissolve gelatin in boiling water. Add lemon juice and salt. Chill till partially set. Fold in cottage cheese. Pour into 5 or 6 individual ring molds. Chill till set. Unmold on lettuce. Fill centers with mayonnaise and polka dot with capers. Arrange shrimp as shown.

Vary basic salad with these six seafoods, or with the specialties of your region

Tuna is packed in 6½- and 7-ounce (1 cup) and 9¼-ounce (1½ cups) cans; *salmon* in 7¾-ounce (1 cup) and 1-pound (2 cups) cans.

Buy *scallops* frozen in 1-pound (1 cup cooked) or 12-ounce packages.

Buy *crab* alive; in 6½- or 7½-ounce cans (about 1 cup); or frozen cooked—packaged or in shell. A 2-pound crab contains 2 cups cooked meat. Buy *lobster* in 5-ounce cans.

Or cook frozen *lobster tails* in shell—2 pounds give you 2⅔ cups cooked meat.

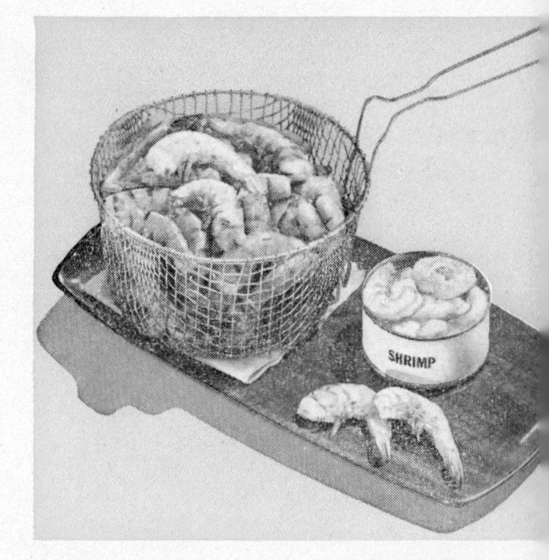

Buy *shrimp* in 4½- or 5-ounce cans (about 1 cup).

Or, for 1 cup cleaned cooked shrimp, buy ¾ pound raw (fresh or frozen) shrimp in shell, or 7 ounces frozen shelled shrimp.

Clam Mountain

1 7- or 7½-ounce can (about 1 cup) minced clams
1 clove garlic
1 8-ounce package cream cheese, softened
1 teaspoon lemon juice
1 teaspoon Worcestershire sauce
½ teaspoon salt
Dash pepper
• • •
6 to 8 green-pepper rings, cut ½ inch thick
Cucumber slices
Minced parsley

Drain clams. Rub mixing bowl with cut clove of garlic. In bowl, blend cream cheese, lemon juice, Worcestershire sauce, salt, pepper, and clams. Chill.

Place green-pepper rings on salad plates and fill halfway with cucumber slices; top with clam mixture. Sprinkle generously with parsley. Serve as appetizer dip or salad, with radish accordions and crackers.

Makes 6 to 8 servings.

Grapefruit-Shrimp Salad in Avocado Ring Mold

1 package lemon-flavored gelatin
1 cup boiling water
1 cup mayonnaise or salad dressing
1 to 2 tablespoons lemon juice
1 teaspoon salt
1 cup peeled, sieved avocado
1 cup heavy cream, whipped
• • •
1½ cups grapefruit sections, halved or whole
2 cups cooked cleaned shrimp
1 cup diced celery
2 tablespoons lemon juice
⅓ cup clear French dressing, or ¾ cup mayonnaise
½ teaspoon celery salt

Dissolve gelatin in boiling water. Chill till partially set. Whip till fluffy. Stir in mayonnaise, lemon juice, and salt. Fold in avocado and whipped cream. Pour into 1½-quart ring mold or 6 individual ring molds. Chill till firm.

Drain grapefruit sections. Add remaining ingredients and toss lightly. Chill.

Unmold avocado rings on chilled plates. Fill centers with grapefruit-shrimp mixture. Trim with curly endive and lemon wedges.

Makes 6 servings.

Dress up seafood salad in a jiffy

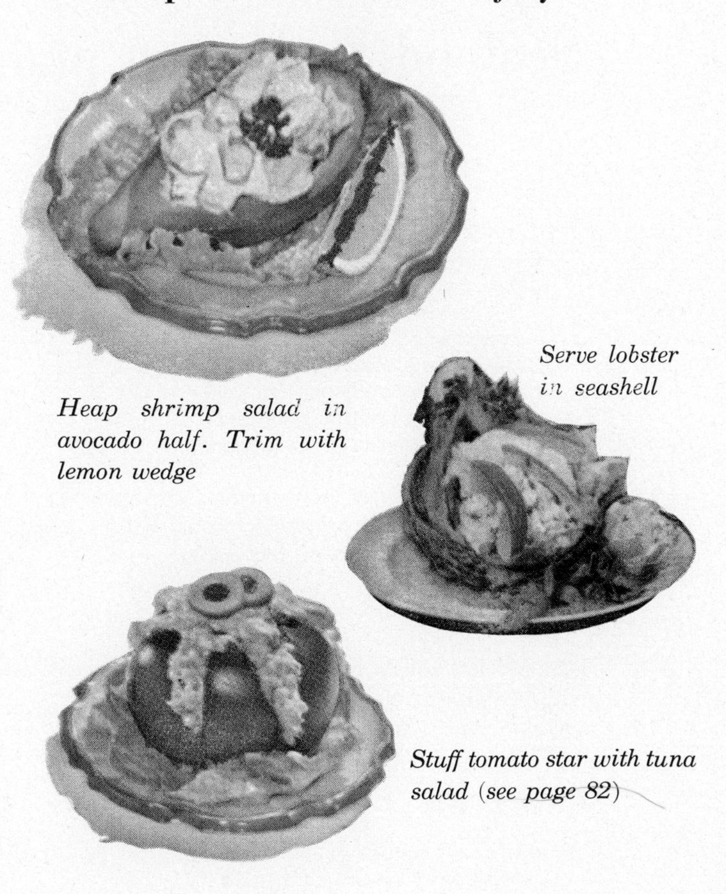

Heap shrimp salad in avocado half. Trim with lemon wedge

Serve lobster in seashell

Stuff tomato star with tuna salad (see page 82)

Try these as appetizers, dinner salads

Capers add dash to Shrimp With Lime Rings

Clam Mountain is salad and dip!

Seafood, turkey go plain or fancy in salad

Lobster and Orange Cup

1 5-ounce can (1 cup) lobster, flaked
¼ teaspoon salt
3 large oranges, pared and sectioned
• • •
¼ cup orange juice
2 tablespoons mayonnaise
¼ teaspoon grated orange peel
½ cup heavy cream, whipped
Prepared horseradish to taste

Break lobster in ½-inch pieces; sprinkle with salt. Toss with orange sections. Chill.

To make dressing, combine orange juice, mayonnaise, and peel; fold in whipped cream and add horseradish.

Heap chilled lobster mixture in individual lettuce-lined bowls or sherbet glasses. Pass whipped-cream dressing, and nutmeg to sprinkle over. Makes 4 servings.

Crab Louis

1 cup mayonnaise or salad dressing
¼ cup heavy cream, whipped
¼ cup chili sauce
¼ cup chopped green pepper
¼ cup chopped green onion and tops
1 teaspoon lemon juice
• • •
1 large head lettuce
2 to 3 cups cooked crab meat, or 2 6½-ounce cans, chilled
2 large tomatoes, cut in wedges
2 hard-cooked eggs, cut in wedges

Combine mayonnaise, whipped cream, chili sauce, green pepper, green onion, and lemon juice. Salt to taste. Chill. Makes 2 cups of Louis Dressing.

Line four large plates with lettuce leaves. Shred rest of lettuce, arrange on leaves.

Remove bits of shell from crab meat. Reserve claw meat; leave remainder in chunks and arrange atop lettuce. Circle with wedges of tomato and egg. Sprinkle with salt. Pour ¼ cup Louis Dressing over each salad. Sprinkle with paprika. Top with claw meat. Pass remaining dressing.

Makes 4 servings.

Green Goddess Salad

1 cup mayonnaise or salad dressing
2 tablespoons anchovy paste
1 teaspoon Worcestershire sauce
½ teaspoon dry mustard
1 clove garlic, minced
3 tablespoons chopped chives or green onions
2 tablespoons finely chopped cooked cleaned shrimp
1 hard-cooked egg, finely chopped
• • •
½ head romaine
1 bunch leaf lettuce
1 cup cooked cleaned shrimp, chilled
1 stalk French endive, sliced
3 medium tomatoes, quartered
½ cup julienne-style cooked beets, drained and chilled

Combine mayonnaise, anchovy paste, Worcestershire sauce, dry mustard, and garlic. Stir in chives, chopped shrimp, and egg. Chill. Makes 1½ cups Green Goddess Dressing.

Break up romaine and leaf lettuce in bite-size pieces. Place on salad plates. Arrange shrimp, endive, tomatoes, and beets atop. Spoon dressing over. Makes 6 to 8 servings.

Hot Tuna-Macaroni Toss

½ 7-ounce package (1 cup) elbow macaroni
¼ cup Italian dressing
1 teaspoon celery seed
¾ teaspoon dry mustard
½ teaspoon salt
Dash pepper
• • •
1 6½-ounce can (1 cup) tuna, flaked
½ cup diced celery
½ cup diced green pepper
3 tablespoons mayonnaise

Cook macaroni in boiling salted water till tender; drain. In skillet, mix Italian dressing and seasonings; heat just to boiling. Add macaroni, tuna, celery, and green pepper. Toss lightly and heat just through.

Stir in the salad dressing. Top with green-pepper rings; serve at once. Serves 6.

Turkey-Green Grape Salad

1½ cups diced cooked turkey
1 cup thinly sliced celery
½ cup green seedless grapes
½ cup mayonnaise

Combine turkey, celery, grapes, and mayonnaise. Season to taste with salt and pepper. Toss lightly. Serve on greens and trim with small bunch of grapes. Or serve in avocado halves brushed with lemon juice.
Makes 6 servings.

Holiday Turkey Salad

2 cups diced cooked or canned turkey
1 cup sliced celery
1 9-ounce can (1 cup) pineapple tidbits, drained
½ cup pomegranate seeds
½ cup slivered blanched almonds, toasted
Mayonnaise to moisten

Combine ingredients; toss lightly. Serve on lettuce. Pass mayonnaise. Makes 6 servings.

Hearty Turkey-Apple Toss

2 tablespoons lemon juice, fresh, frozen, or canned
2 cups diced cooked or canned turkey or chicken
½ cup diced apple
1 cup diced celery
2 hard-cooked eggs, chopped
¼ cup chopped blanched almonds, toasted

• • •

⅓ cup mayonnaise or salad dressing
½ teaspoon salt
Dash pepper
½ teaspoon sweet basil

Sprinkle lemon juice over turkey and apple; toss lightly. Add celery, egg, and almonds.
Blend mayonnaise and seasonings; fold into turkey mixture. Serve in lettuce cups and trim with additional apple slices.
Or, spoon into ring of Cheesed Tomato Aspic, (page 91). Pass hot rolls.
Makes about 4 cups of salad.

Shrimp-Cucumber Crisp is a quick summer speciality

Cucumbers, heads of Bibb lettuce (one to a salad), and cooked cleaned shrimp wait in the refrigerator.
At mealtime, place a head of Bibb (leave it whole) in each salad bowl. Nestle pink shrimp (split in half for easier, daintier eating) and crispy green-rimmed cucumber slices among the leaves.
Dress salad with oil and vinegar, or mayonnaise polka-dotted with capers.
Make it a meal by passing egg-salad sandwiches, one-bite cherry tomatoes, iced coffee. For dessert—a fruit-cheese plate and more coffee.

Lazy-cook a chicken for salad

Buy a 3½- to 5-pound ready-to-cook stewing chicken or "bro-hen" (an older broiler-fryer). Buy pieces, or cut up whole hen. Place back, wings, legs on bottom of Dutch oven. More tender white meat goes on top to steam-cook.

Add water now—about ½ cup per pound, when cooking chicken for salad use.

(Water turns to rich broth as chicken cooks. Cool chicken in it, then refrigerate immediately. Use later with noodles; in gravy.)

Add stalk of celery, a carrot, an onion, 1 whole clove, 2 whole black peppers, salt—½ teaspoon per pound of chicken. Bring to boiling; reduce heat. Cover. *Simmer* 2½ to 4 hours or till thickest piece is fork-tender.

Basic Chicken Salad

Combine 3 cups diced cooked or canned chicken and 2 cups diced celery.

To ½ cup mayonnaise or salad dressing, add ¼ cup chopped pickle, 3 tablespoons lemon juice, 1 teaspoon seasoned salt, and ¼ teaspoon pepper. Pour mixture over chicken and celery. Let chill 1 hour.

Serve in lettuce cups. Trim with slices of ripe olive or hard-cooked egg. Serves 4 to 6.

Fruited Chicken Salad

3 cups diced cooked or canned chicken
1 cup diced celery
1 cup orange sections
1 9-ounce can (1 cup) pineapple tidbits, drained
½ cup slivered almonds, toasted
2 tablespoons salad oil
2 tablespoons orange juice
2 tablespoons vinegar
½ teaspoon salt
Dash marjoram
½ cup mayonnaise or salad dressing

Combine first 5 ingredients. Blend salad oil, orange juice, vinegar, and seasonings. Add to chicken mixture. Chill 1 hour. Drain. Add mayonnaise; toss. Makes 8 to 10 servings.

Chicken Salad in Raspberry Ring

2 cups cubed cooked or canned chicken
¾ cup sliced celery
2 hard-cooked eggs, chopped
1 teaspoon lemon juice
¼ teaspoon salt
½ cup Creamy Mayonnaise (page 134)

• • •

2 10-ounce packages frozen raspberries
2 envelopes unflavored gelatin
¾ cup sugar
¼ teaspoon salt
1¼ cups boiling water
½ cup lemon juice
1½ cups small cantaloupe balls

Lightly toss first 6 ingredients. Chill.

Thaw and sieve raspberries. Add enough water to make 2 cups. Combine gelatin, sugar, and salt. Add boiling water, stirring to dissolve. Stir in lemon juice and sieved raspberries. Chill till partially set. Fold in cantaloupe; pour into 6-cup ring mold. Chill firm.

Unmold gelatin ring on greens. Fill with chilled chicken salad.

Chicken Salad in Raspberry Ring stars in "party pink" buffet

Supper's extra special when you serve this hearty salad in a rosy ring full of watermelon balls! For fun, carry out the color scheme—pass pink lemonade (easy with frozen concentrate); decorate with pink daisies, napkins, mats.

Round out the meal with Bran Muffins (page 151), cream-cheese-stuffed celery, nuts—*and* pink ice cream.

Curried Chicken in Pepper Cups

6 medium green peppers

• • •

1⅓ cups packaged precooked rice
2 cups diced canned or cooked chicken
1 cup chopped celery
¼ cup minced onion
2 tablespoons chopped canned pimiento

• • •

1 cup mayonnaise or salad dressing
1 teaspoon curry powder
½ teaspoon salt
Dash pepper

Remove tops and seeds from peppers; partially cook in small amount boiling salted water, about 5 minutes; drain.

Prepare rice according to package directions; mix with chicken, celery, onion, and pimiento. Combine mayonnaise, salad dressing and seasonings; add to rice mixture and toss lightly.

Fill peppers and place in greased 10x6x1½-inch baking dish; pour small amount of water around peppers. Bake in moderate oven (350°) about 30 minutes or till peppers are tender. Makes 6 servings.

Chicken in Cheese Shell

1½ cups sifted enriched flour
½ teaspoon salt
½ cup shortening
½ cup shredded sharp process American cheese
4 to 5 tablespoons cold water

• • •

1½ cups diced cooked or canned chicken
1 9-ounce can (1 cup) pineapple tidbits, drained
1 cup chopped California walnuts
½ cup sliced celery

• • •

1 cup dairy sour cream
⅔ cup salad dressing

Make a cheese pastry shell of first five ingredients, adding ⅓ *cup* of cheese with the shortening (save remaining cheese for topping). Bake in 8-inch piepan. Cool.

Combine chicken, pineapple, nuts, and celery. Blend sour cream and mayonnaise and add ⅔ *cup* to chicken mixture; mix well. Spoon into pastry shell. Top with remaining sour-cream mixture. Sprinkle with reserved cheese. Chill. Trim with ripe-olive slices. Makes 6 servings.

Chicken-Cranberry Layers

Cranberry layer:

1 envelope (1 tablespoon) unflavored gelatin
¼ cup cold water
1 1-pound can (2 cups) whole cranberry sauce
1 9-ounce can (1 cup) crushed pineapple
½ cup broken California walnuts
1 tablespoon lemon juice

Soften gelatin in cold water. Dissolve over hot water. Add remaining ingredients. Pour into 10x6x1½-inch baking dish; chill firm.

Chicken layer:

1 envelope (1 tablespoon) unflavored gelatin
¼ cup cold water
1 cup mayonnaise or salad dressing
½ cup water
3 tablespoons lemon juice
¾ teaspoon salt
2 cups diced cooked or canned chicken
½ cup diced celery
2 tablespoons chopped parsley

Soften gelatin in ¼ cup cold water. Dissolve over hot water. Blend in mayonnaise, ½ cup water, lemon juice, and salt. Add chicken, celery, and parsley. Pour over cranberry layer; chill till firm.

Cut in 6 to 8 squares; invert on lettuce. Top with mayonnaise and walnut halves.

Chicken Buffet Molds

1 envelope (1 tablespoon) unflavored gelatin
½ cup cold water
1 cup mayonnaise or salad dressing
1½ cups diced cooked or canned chicken
½ cup chopped unpared cucumber
⅓ cup diced celery
3 tablespoons minced onion
3 tablespoons chopped green olives
1 tablespoon diced pimiento
2 tablespoons lemon juice
½ teaspoon salt
¼ teaspoon paprika
1 cup heavy cream, whipped

Soften gelatin in cold water. Dissolve over hot water; stir into mayonnaise. Stir in remaining ingredients except cream. Fold in whipped cream. Pour into 8 individual molds; chill firm. Unmold. Trim with ripe-olive whirligigs, pimiento (see page 94).

Like to fix most of summer supper early? Plan meal around these hearty make-ahead salads

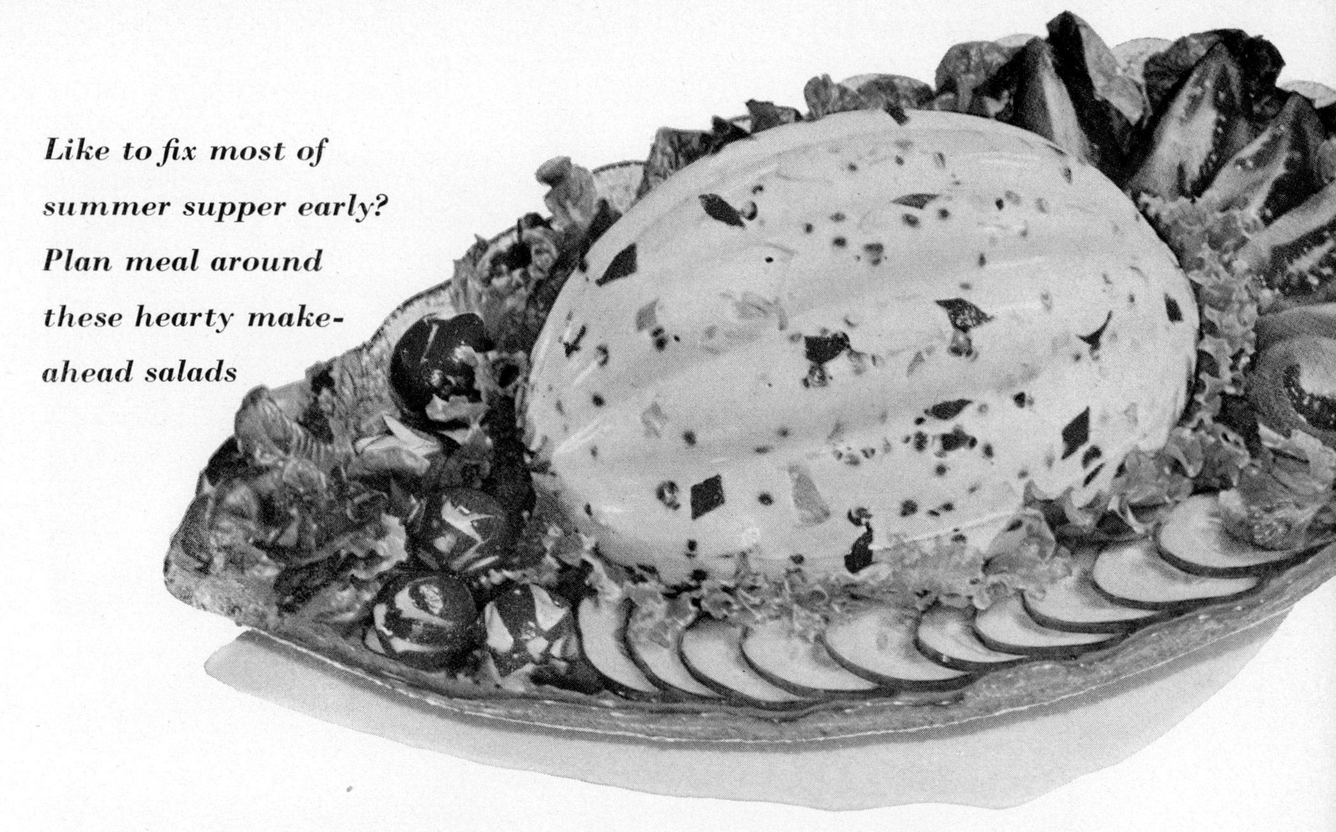

Snowy Chicken Confetti Salad is pretty as a picture—creamy white with flecks of pimiento and green pepper. Frame it with a lettuce ruffle, tomato wedges, green-rimmed cucumber slices, radish roses. Pass Parmesan Toast Strips (page 156), fruit punch, canned-peach shortcake.

Try meats in chilly molded salads

Jellied Chicken Almond

1 envelope (1 tablespoon) unflavored gelatin
¼ cup cold water

• • •

1 cup mayonnaise
1 cup heavy cream, whipped
½ teaspoon salt

• • •

1½ cups diced cooked or canned chicken
¾ cup chopped blanched almonds, toasted
¾ cup halved green seedless grapes

Soften gelatin in cold water; dissolve over hot water. Cool slightly; combine with mayonnaise, whipped cream, and salt. Fold in remaining ingredients. Spoon into 6 to 8 individual molds; chill till firm. Unmold on lettuce. Trim with stuffed olive slices, peaks of mayonnaise (see picture, page 143).

Snowy Chicken Confetti Salad

2 envelopes (2 tablespoons) unflavored gelatin
½ cup cold water
1 can condensed chicken consomme

• • •

1 cup mayonnaise
2½ cups diced cooked or canned chicken
½ cup diced green pepper
½ cup diced celery
½ cup diced pimiento
¼ cup lemon juice
¼ teaspoon salt

• • •

1 cup heavy cream, whipped

Soften gelatin in cold water. Dissolve in hot consomme. Chill until partially set.

Stir in remaining ingredients except cream. Fold in whipped cream. Pour into 1½-quart mold. Chill till firm. Serves 10.

Ham Loaf has glamorous stripes of pimiento and sieved, hard-cooked egg yolk and white. Help yourself to deviled eggs, potato salad in aspic ring, fruit kabobs. Relishes, hot rolls make the rounds later.

How to make the "meat" look like a party!

Corned-beef Salad Mold

1 envelope unflavored gelatin
¼ cup cold water
1½ cups boiling tomato juice
2 teaspoons lemon juice
½ teaspoon salt
1 12-ounce can corned beef, crumbled
½ cup chopped celery
½ cup chopped cucumber
1 tablespoon chopped onion
1 cup mayonnaise

Soften gelatin in cold water; dissolve in tomato juice. Add lemon juice; salt. Chill till partially set. Fold in other ingredients. Chill firm in an 8½x4½x2½-inch loaf pan. Unmold. Serve with deviled eggs. Serves 8.

Ham Loaf

1 5-pound smoked picnic
2 envelopes unflavored gelatin
3 cups boiling ham stock
1 bouillon cube (*omit if stock is salty*)
2 tablespoons prepared horseradish
1 tablespoon prepared mustard

Remove skin from picnic. Place in large pan, cover with water. Simmer, covered, about 3 hours. Remove meat from bone; put enough through food chopper (coarse blade) to make 5 cups. Soften gelatin in ½ *cup cold water;* dissolve in hot stock; stir in bouillon cube, horseradish, and mustard. Cool; add meat.

Pour into a 9½x5x3-inch loaf pan. Chill firm. Unmold. Makes 8 to 10 servings.

Party Ham Ring

1 envelope (1 tablespoon) unflavored gelatin
¼ cup cold water
¾ cup boiling water
1 cup dairy sour cream
½ cup mayonnaise or salad dressing
3 tablespoons vinegar
¼ teaspoon salt
Dash pepper
• • •
1½ cups diced cooked or canned ham
1 cup celery slices
¼ cup chopped green pepper
3 tablespoons chopped green onions

Soften gelatin in cold water; dissolve in boiling water. Blend in sour cream, mayonnaise, vinegar, salt, and pepper. Chill till partially set; whip until fluffy. Fold in remaining ingredients. Pour into 5½-cup ring mold. Chill till firm. Makes 5 to 6 servings.

Tangy Tuna Mousse Squares

2 envelopes (2 tablespoons) unflavored gelatin
½ cup cold water
1 cup mayonnaise
2 6½- or 7-ounce cans (2 cups) tuna, flaked
½ cup diced celery
¼ cup chopped stuffed green olives
1 tablespoon finely chopped onion
2 tablespoons lemon juice
1½ teaspoons prepared horseradish
¼ teaspoon salt
¼ teaspoon paprika
1 cup heavy cream, whipped

Soften gelatin in cold water; dissolve over boiling water; stir into mayonnaise. Add remaining ingredients except cream. Mix well. Fold in whipped cream. Pour into 10x6x1½-inch pan. Chill till firm. Cut in squares and serve on greens. Makes 8 to 10 servings.

Try ham this way

Party Ham Ring is a picture of good eating. Sour cream for piquant flavor, ham for heartiness, celery, green pepper, onion for crispness.

Those are slices of smoked cheese roll in the tomatoes.

Shrimp-Lime Double Decker

High-and-handsome stack-up holds shrimp in tomato aspic and cottage cheese in lime gelatin. Trim with extra shrimp, deviled eggs, Bibb lettuce. Pass chili sauce, chived sour cream.

Shrimp-Lime Double Decker

Lime layer:

1 package lime-flavored gelatin
1½ cups boiling water
1 12-ounce carton (1½ cups) large-curd cream-style cottage cheese, drained
1½ teaspoons chopped onion
1½ teaspoons lemon juice or vinegar
2 tablespoons prepared horseradish
1 tablespoon mayonnaise

Dissolve gelatin in boiling water. Chill till partially set. Beat till light. Stir in remaining ingredients; pour into 1½-quart mold or 8½x4½x2½-inch loaf pan. Chill till set.

Shrimp aspic layer:

1 1-pound can (2 cups) tomatoes
¼ cup chopped onion
3 tablespoons chopped celery leaves
1 bay leaf
1 whole clove
1 tablespoon brown sugar
½ teaspoon salt

• • •

1 envelope unflavored gelatin
3 tablespoons cold water
3 tablespoons lemon juice
1 cup cleaned cooked or canned shrimp

Combine first 7 ingredients; simmer 5 minutes. Strain. Soften gelatin in cold water; dissolve in hot tomato mixture. Add lemon juice. Chill aspic till partially set.

Dip shrimp in the aspic; arrange against side of mold, atop firmly set lime layer; chill till set. Pour in remaining aspic. Chill firm. Unmold on greens. Makes 8 to 10 servings.

Peppy Shrimp Ring

2 envelopes unflavored gelatin
½ cup cold water
1½ teaspoons salt
¼ cup catsup
2 cups dairy sour cream
¼ cup lemon juice
¼ cup prepared horseradish
3 cups cooked cleaned shrimp, in pieces
1 cup chopped green pepper
1 cup chopped celery

Soften gelatin in cold water; dissolve over hot water; cool slightly. Combine salt, catsup, sour cream, lemon juice, and horseradish; add to gelatin. Add remaining ingredients. Pour into 5-cup ring mold. Chill till firm. Unmold. Makes 6 servings.

Lemony Salmon Tower

Lemon layer:

1 envelope (1 tablespoon) unflavored gelatin
¼ cup cold water
1 cup boiling water
1 tablespoon sugar
½ teaspoon salt
3 tablespoons lemon juice
Few drops yellow food coloring

Soften gelatin in cold water. Dissolve in boiling water. Add sugar, salt, lemon juice, and food coloring. Pour into 2½-quart mold. Chill until set.

Salmon-salad layer:

3 envelopes unflavored gelatin
¾ cup cold water
3¼ cups boiling water
¼ cup vinegar
¼ cup lemon juice
1½ teaspoons salt
2 1-pound cans (4 cups) red salmon, drained and broken in pieces
2 cups drained canned or cooked peas
1½ cups diced celery
½ cup green-pepper strips
½ cup thinly sliced unpared cucumber

Soften gelatin in cold water. Dissolve in boiling water. Add vinegar, lemon juice, and salt. Chill till partially set. Add salmon and vegetables; mix carefully. Pour over lemon layer. Chill firm. Makes 12 servings.

Tuna Crunch Loaf

2 envelopes unflavored gelatin
½ cup cold water
1 can condensed cream of celery soup
¼ cup lemon juice
1 tablespoon prepared mustard
1 teaspoon salt
Dash pepper
1 cup mayonnaise or salad dressing
2 6½-ounce cans (2 cups) tuna, flaked
1 cup chopped celery
½ cup grated cucumber
¼ cup chopped green pepper

Soften gelatin in cold water. Heat soup just to boiling; add gelatin and stir to dissolve. Stir in lemon juice, mustard, salt, and pepper. Chill till partially set. Add mayonnaise. Fold in tuna, celery, cucumber, and green pepper. Pour into 8½x4½x2½-inch loaf pan. Chill firm. Unmold. Makes 8 servings.

Lemony Salmon Towers, stars on salad tray

Tart shimmery lemon gelatin accents rich salmon flavor in this luscious molded salad. Cucumber, celery, green pepper add crunch. Relishes are anchovies, herring in sour cream, marinated shrimp, sardines, pickled beets, and pickles.

PEPPER
SALT

Egg and cheese salads

Salad eggs (or deviled)—that favorite of the good old lazy picnic, or family supper and sophisticated smorgasbord—who doesn't like to bite into their cool, smooth, and golden goodness? It behooves the cook to know all the tricks along the way: How to cook an egg tender, shell it easily, slice it neatly. All this is on page 119, plus the fun of tinting hard-cooked eggs in beautiful Easter colors.

But not all *egg* salads are *salad* eggs. Look left for egg salad in glamorous "shell" of crusty Vienna bread. For salads in a bowl, there's one with cool lettuce chunks, sliced hard-cooked eggs, thin crisp rings of sweet onion, and a dressing of oil and vinegar, fresh seasonings, some sharp cheese. Another calls for greens, bright spring radishes and onions, crisp bacon bits. A make-ahead, Egg-Cheese Souffle Salad has the refreshing lightness of a gelatin salad, the sturdy good eating of eggs and cheese.

Cheese adds country-style freshness, creamy richness

Cottage cheese good as is—fresh-tasting, cool, snow-white—is the start of many a fine salad. Ever stir in sour cream, some cuke and radish and onion, then serve it in lettuce-lined bowl, or in plump tomato cups? That's just *one* idea. Read the rest. Cottage cheese is perfect, too, for the lovely gelatin salads that happily stand by while you're on other business.

When you open a package of cream cheese and get out the whipping cream you're getting into the elegant class of the ladies' luncheon. The I-have-the-most-wonderful-new-recipe class. And wonderful's the word. Look at the salad beauties on pages 124 and 125. Just to read the recipes with their fresh summer fruits and rich cheese and crunchy nuts is to anticipate the lushness you behold in the pictures. If you haven't the fancy molds, no need to pass up the treat. Use your custard cups—the flavor's the same! See the delicious *frozen* salads, too.

Fruit or vegetable, the salad's not made that isn't made better with the tang or the mellowness of cheese. Have it ready to shred, to crumble, to cut in sticks or cubes; or blend it into the salad itself.

Humpty Dumpty Salad: Hot idea for a summertime supper

← Slice through deliciously seasoned egg salad, hot, crusty Vienna loaf. For the taking are dill pickles, little radishes, stuffed olives, Carrot Crisps. Let each one brush hot melted butter onto a steaming golden ear; then relax and enjoy summer's breeze, summer's bounty. The salad (page 119) is diced hard-cooked eggs, chopped olives, a bit of onion and garlic, some crumbs hollowed from the loaf, mayonnaise pepped up with mustard. You fill the loaf with salad, brush the crust with butter. Foil-wrap; bake briefly to heat through.

Deviled-egg "daisies" make pretty trim In the mood for spring? Why not turn Deviled Eggs into dainty white-and-gold flowers? Notch small end of egg to make petal-like opening. Remove yolks and make filling. Refill whites, using pastry tube. If egg "wobbles" cut thin slice off base. Chill.

Delicious, health-wise egg salads

Deviled Eggs

6 hard-cooked eggs, halved lengthwise
¼ cup mayonnaise
¼ teaspoon salt
Dash pepper
2 teaspoons prepared mustard
1 tablespoon minced onion
1 tablespoon *finely* chopped celery (optional)
1 tablespoon finely chopped stuffed green olives (optional)*

Remove egg yolks. Mash, and combine with remaining ingredients. Refill egg whites, using pastry tube if desired. Chill. Trim tops with pimiento diamonds or paprika.

(For plump Deviled Eggs, refill only 8 halves; chop extras and use for tomato-salad trim next day.)

*Or, substitute crumbled bacon, chopped pimiento, chives, sweet pickle, or parsley.

Old-fashioned Egg Salad

1 head lettuce
6 hard-cooked eggs, sliced
1 small onion, thinly sliced

• • •

½ cup salad oil
¼ cup vinegar
2 teaspoons Worcestershire sauce
½ cup shredded sharp American cheese
2 tablespoons snipped parsley
½ teaspoon salt
½ teaspoon pepper
Dash paprika

Break lettuce into salad bowl in bite-size pieces. Alternate layers of egg and onion.

Make dressing of salad oil, vinegar, Worcestershire sauce, cheese, parsley, and seasonings. Pour over salad in bowl. Toss lightly; serve. Makes 6 servings.

Bacon and Egg Toss

½ clove garlic, minced
⅓ cup clear French dressing

• • •

3 cups torn lettuce
2 cups torn curly endive
8 slices bacon, fried and drained
¼ cup chopped green onions and tops
½ cup sliced celery
⅓ cup sliced radishes
2 tomatoes, cut in wedges
4 hard-cooked eggs, sliced

Add minced garlic to dressing.

Place greens in salad bowl and crumble 6 of the slices of bacon atop. Add onions, celery, and radishes. Pour dressing over and toss. Add tomatoes and egg slices (reserve some for trim if desired); toss *very* lightly.

Crumble remaining strips of bacon over. Makes 6 servings.

Hot Humpty-dumpty Salad In Bread Boat

1 loaf Vienna bread

• • •

6 hard-cooked eggs, coarsely diced
1½ cups diced celery
½ cup chopped stuffed green olives
¼ cup chopped onion
1 clove garlic, minced
¾ teaspoon salt
¼ teaspoon pepper

• • •

½ cup mayonnaise
2 tablespoons prepared mustard

• • •

Melted butter or margarine

Cut top crust off bread and reserve for lid. Hollow out loaf to within 1 inch of bottom. Crumble enough bread (taken from center) to make 1 cup crumbs; add eggs, celery, olives, onion, garlic, and seasonings.

Combine mayonnaise and mustard; add to egg mixture and toss lightly. Fill "boat"; replace top; brush loaf with butter. Wrap in foil. Bake in hot oven (425°) 30 to 35 minutes, or till heated through. Top salad with egg and olive slices.

To match picture on page 116, serve on tray with lettuce cups filled with dill-pickle sticks, rosy radishes, stuffed green olives and Carrot Crisps (page 71).

Cut loaf in 8 slices and serve hot with buttered roasting ears, steaming coffee.

Egg-Cheese Souffle Salad

1 package lemon-flavored gelatin
1 cup boiling water
½ cup cold water
½ cup mayonnaise
1 tablespoon lemon juice
¾ teaspoon salt
3 or 4 drops Tabasco sauce

• • •

¾ cup shredded American cheese
3 or 4 hard-cooked eggs, sliced
½ cup diced celery
¼ cup diced green pepper
2 tablespoons diced pimiento
1 teaspoon grated onion

Dissolve gelatin in boiling water. Add cold water, mayonnaise, lemon juice, salt, and Tabasco. Blend well with electric or rotary beater. Quick-chill in freezing unit 15 to 20 minutes, or till firm 1 inch from edge.

Turn into bowl and beat till fluffy. Fold in remaining ingredients. Pour into 1-quart mold or individual molds. Chill till firm, 30 to 60 minutes. Unmold on greens. Serve with thick slices of ham, crisp potato chips. Makes 6 servings.

Cook, cool eggs for salad this way; color some for fun

Place eggs in saucepan and cover with cold water (at least 1 inch above eggs). Bring to boiling; reduce heat. Cover; cook just below simmering 15 to 20 minutes.

Cool eggs *promptly* in cold water, to stop cooking and make shelling easier.

For uniform slices, use an egg slicer. For wedges, divide egg with another simple tool —a small metal wheel with taut wire "spokes."

Make pretty holidaytime salad garnishes by tinting shelled, hard-cooked eggs with summer-drink powder. Dissolve each envelope of the flavored drink powder in 1 cup water—mix enough to cover eggs.

Put in peeled hard-cooked eggs; let stand till desired color. Dry tinted eggs on a rack. Make these into Deviled Egg "daisies" (see picture, opposite page)—pretty for an Easter luncheon! Or send whole in a lunch-box—children will be delighted.

Plan luncheons around cheese salads

Cheese-Peach "Sandwiches"

To softened cream cheese, add chopped walnuts and cut-up dates; blend. "Sandwich" two chilled canned peach halves (drained) together with mixture. Serve on greens with strawberries to match cover.

Sour Cream-Cottage Cheese Garden Salad

2 cups dairy sour cream
2 cups large-curd, cream-style cottage cheese
¾ cup diced cucumber
½ cup sliced radishes
½ cup sliced green onions
¾ teaspoon salt

Blend sour cream with cottage cheese. Stir in chilled vegetables, salt, dash of pepper.

Serve in lettuce-lined bowl; trim with green-pepper rings. Or, spoon into tomato cups. Makes 6 to 8 servings.

Macaroni-and-Cheese Salad in Pepper Cups is spiked with mustard, onion, sweet pickle; decked in zigzagged green jacket. Cubes of Cheddar and ham make it a main dish.

Cottage Cheese Coleslaw

½ cup cream-style cottage cheese
½ cup mayonnaise or salad dressing
2 tablespoons vinegar
½ teaspoon caraway seed
½ teaspoon onion juice
¼ teaspoon Worcestershire sauce
8 cups finely shredded chilled cabbage

Combine cottage cheese and mayonnaise; add vinegar, caraway seed, onion juice, and Worcestershire. Toss this dressing lightly with cabbage. For stronger caraway flavor, chill several hours.

Serve slaw in large bowl lined with cabbage leaves. Makes 6 to 8 servings.

Macaroni-and-Cheese Salad in Pepper Cups

½ 7-ounce package (about 1 cup) 7-minute macaroni

• • •

6 medium green peppers
2 cups diced canned or cooked ham
¼ pound sharp Cheddar cheese, diced
¼ cup diced sweet pickle
2 tablespoons chopped pimiento
2 tablespoons minced onion

• • •

½ cup mayonnaise or salad dressing
2 teaspoons prepared mustard
¼ teaspoon salt

Cook macaroni in boiling salted water till tender; drain and cool.

Cut off pepper tops, making large zigzags. Remove seeds and membrane.* (If desired, precook in boiling salted water 5 minutes; plunge immediately in cold water, then peel.)

Chop enough green-pepper scraps to make ⅓ cup. Combine with macaroni, ham, cheese, pickle, pimiento, and onion.

Blend together mayonnaise, mustard, and salt; combine with the macaroni mixture. Sprinkle inside of pepper cups with salt and fill with the salad. Chill.

Serve on salad greens with egg wedges. Top with radish roses. Makes 6 servings.

*If uncooked pepper cups are used, first cut sliver off bottom of "wobbly" ones.

Applesauce-Cheese Ribbons

Applesauce-lime layers:

1 1-pound can (2 cups) sweetened applesauce
⅔ cup water
1 package lime-flavored gelatin
2 tablespoons lemon juice

Combine applesauce and water; heat to boiling. Add gelatin and lemon juice; stir to dissolve. Cool. Reserve half of mixture; pour remainder in 1½-quart mold. Chill firm.

Cheese layer:

1 envelope unflavored gelatin
2 tablespoons cold water
¼ cup boiling water
1 12-ounce carton (1½ cups) small-curd cream-style cottage cheese, sieved
1 3-ounce package softened cream cheese
¼ cup mayonnaise or salad dressing
½ cup diced celery

Soften gelatin in cold water; dissolve in boiling water. Blend cheeses and salad dressing; add gelatin and celery; mix well. Pour into mold over firm applesauce layer. Chill firm.

Pour reserved applesauce mixture over cheese layer. Chill firm. Makes 8 servings.

Shrimp In Cottage Cheese Mold

2 packages lime-flavored gelatin
3 cups boiling water
2 12-ounce cartons (3 cups) large-curd cream-style cottage cheese, drained
¼ cup prepared horseradish
2 tablespoons mayonnaise
1 tablespoon vinegar or lemon juice
1 tablespoon chopped onion
1 to 2 cups cooked cleaned shrimp

Dissolve gelatin in boiling water. Chill till partially set. Beat till fluffy. Stir in remaining ingredients. Pour in chilled 6-cup ring mold. Chill firm. Unmold; fill with chilled shrimp, water cress. Makes 8 to 10 servings.

"One-cup" Cottage Ring

Dissolve 1 package lime-flavored gelatin in 1 cup boiling water. Chill until partially set. Blend in 1 cup mayonnaise or salad dressing. Fold in 1 cup chopped celery, 1 cup diced green pepper, and 1 cup large-curd cream-style cottage cheese.

Pour into a 4-cup ring mold. Chill till firm. Unmold on lettuce. Makes 6 servings.

Cheese-Aspic Peaks, with mayonnaise, perky pimiento atop.

Cheese-Aspic Peaks

Cheese topper:

1 3-ounce package cream cheese
¼ cup mayonnaise
¼ teaspoon salt
2 envelopes unflavored gelatin
2 teaspoons lemon juice
2 tablespoons boiling water
¼ cup finely chopped celery
1 tablespoon chopped chives

Blend softened cream cheese, mayonnaise, salt. Soften ½ *teaspoon* gelatin in lemon juice; dissolve in boiling water. Mix remaining ingredients. Pour in 6 individual molds. Chill firm.

Aspic layer:

¼ cup cold water
1 cup boiling water
2 8-ounce cans (2 cups) seasoned tomato sauce
2 tablespoons lemon juice
1 teaspoon salt

Soften ½ *teaspoon* gelatin in cold water; dissolve in boiling water. Add remaining ingredients; pour over cheese layer. Chill firm. Unmold.

Easy on you and they dazzle guests

Cheese-Cranberry Squares

2 3-ounce packages cream cheese, softened
¾ cup mayonnaise or salad dressing
1 cup heavy cream, whipped
1 1-pound can (2 cups) jellied cranberry sauce
1 9-ounce can (1 cup) crushed pineapple, drained
½ cup chopped ripe olives
¼ cup chopped celery

Blend cheese and mayonnaise. Fold in whipped cream. Cut cranberry sauce in half crosswise; cut one part in ½-inch cubes and reserve remainder for trim.

Fold cranberry cubes, pineapple, olives, and celery into cheese mixture. Pour into 1-quart refrigerator tray; freeze firm.

Slice reserved cranberry sauce and cut with cooky cutter for trim.

Cut salad in squares and top each with a cranberry cutout; serve on greens. This is especially nice with meat. Makes 6 servings.

Cranberry-Cream Cheese Frosties

1 1-pound can jellied cranberry sauce
2 to 3 tablespoons lemon juice

• • •

1 3-ounce package cream cheese, whipped
¼ cup mayonnaise or salad dressing
¼ cup sifted confectioners' sugar
1 cup chopped California walnuts
1 cup heavy cream, whipped

Crush cranberry sauce with fork. Add lemon juice. Pour into paper cups or 1-quart refrigerator tray. Combine cream cheese, mayonnaise, and sugar; blend well. Add walnuts. Fold in whipped cream and spread over cranberry mixture; freeze firm.

If frozen in paper cups, split cups and peel away gently. If frozen in tray, cut in pie-shaped wedges. Serve on lettuce. (White layer will then be on top; decorate with cutouts of jellied cranberry sauce if desired.)

Makes 6 to 8 servings.

Summer party? Mold Cranberry-Cream Cheese Frosties in cups

Tart frozen cranberry sauce tops rich smooth cream-cheese-and-whipped-cream layer, crunchy with walnuts. Serve with tea sandwiches, refreshing punch.

New version of fruit-cheese tray

Orange-Cream Cheese Cups on pineapple rings are a dainty accompaniment for wedges of honeydew, balls of cantaloupe. Server holds parsley-dotted mayonnaise too. Sprigs of mint and whimsical paper parasols make summery trim.

Pineapple-Cheese Freeze

4 cups tiny marshmallows or ½ pound large (about 32), cut in pieces
1 9-ounce can (1 cup) crushed pineapple
¼ cup shredded pimiento process or American process cheese
¼ cup mayonnaise or salad dressing
½ cup heavy cream, whipped

Combine first four ingredients. Fold in whipped cream. Pour into refrigerator tray; freeze firm, 3 to 4 hours.

Cut in squares and serve on lettuce. Trim with maraschino cherries.

Makes 6 to 7 servings.

Orange-Cream Cheese Cups

1 No. 2½ can (8 slices) sliced pineapple
1 package orange-flavored gelatin
1 8-ounce package cream cheese, softened
¼ cup orange juice
2 tablespoons lemon juice

Drain pineapple, reserving syrup. Add hot water to syrup to make 1½ cups. Bring to boiling; add gelatin and stir to dissolve.

Gradually blend into cream cheese. Stir in fruit juices. Pour into individual molds. Chill till firm. Unmold on pineapple slices.

Serve with assorted fruits as shown above. Makes 8 servings.

Blue-cheese Salad Sherbet

Combine 1½ cups sugar and ¾ cup lemon juice. Blend 4 ounces crumbled blue cheese (about 1 cup), 2½ cups milk, and 1 cup light cream; add to sugar mixture. Pour into refrigerator tray.

Freeze firm; break in chunks and beat with electric beater till smooth (or freeze till partially frozen and beat with rotary beater). Return to tray; freeze firm.

Serve sherbet in small scoops (or squares) on a chilled platter, with fresh fruits.

Makes 10 to 12 servings.

Try many cheeses in salad

Cottage Cheese—Mound on fruit plate or stir into fruit or seafood molds. Blend into dressings.
Cream Cheese—Blend into frozen salads, roll balls in nuts for molded fruit salads, whip for dressings.
Cheddar, Swiss—Cut in strips or cube for salad bowls. Or buy packaged cubed or shredded Cheddar.
Blue, Roquefort—Blend into dressings, sprinkle over salad bowls.
Parmesan—Sprinkle over greens.

Luscious luncheons for company

"Everything's ready on the porch. Come and help yourself!"

That's an invitation to pick a Molded Cheese Snowcap (on pineapple rings) off the platter, follow it with an avocado slice, canned peach half and some ripe strawberries from the center mound of fruit.

Sprinkle flaked coconut over the fruit on your plate, and take your choice of clear Honey Dressing (page 132) or fluffy Lemonade Dressing, near the crackers (page 135).

Pick up crackers, hot rolls as you go by.

Invite the ladies; bring in this fruit-circled cheese special

Want an easy and *good* fix-ahead when you entertain the bridge club? How about Chilly Cheese Mountain, full of green grapes and pecans, cream cheese, cottage cheese, and fluffy whipped cream?

To match picture, garnish this way—split and twist juicy canned pineapple slices between peeled apricots. Fill in with pink-grapefruit sections and ripe strawberry halves, or other fruits in season.

Molded Cheese Snowcaps

1 12-ounce carton (1½ cups) small-curd cream-style cottage cheese
2 3-ounce packages cream cheese

• • •

1 teaspoon unflavored gelatin
¼ cup cold water
¼ teaspoon salt

• • •

1 cup green seedless grapes, halved
½ cup broken pecans
2 tablespoons chopped chives
1 cup heavy cream, whipped
Pineapple slices

Mash cheeses together till well blended.

Soften gelatin in cold water; dissolve over boiling water; add salt. Stir gelatin mixture into cheese mixture.

Add grapes, nuts, and chives. Fold in whipped cream. Spoon into individual molds. Chill 4 to 6 hours.

Unmold on pineapple slices and arrange on leaf lettuce. Serve with assorted fruits.

Makes 6 to 8 servings.

Chilly Cheese Mountain: Double recipe for Molded Cheese Snowcaps, leaving out gelatin, water, and salt.

Add grapes, pecans, and chives directly to cheese mixture. Chill in 2-quart mold. Unmold on lettuce and sprinkle with pistachio nuts. Circle with fruit. Pass mayonnaise. Makes 12 servings. See picture below.

Fruit-Nut Cheese Mold

1 No. 2 can (2½ cups) crushed pineapple
1 package lime-flavored gelatin
2 3-ounce packages cream cheese
⅓ cup chopped pimiento
1 cup heavy cream, whipped
1 cup diced celery
1 cup chopped California walnuts

Heat pineapple to boiling point; add gelatin and stir to dissolve. Chill till partially set. Soften cream cheese; stir in pimiento; add to gelatin mixture and blend. Fold in whipped cream, celery, and nuts. Pour into 1½-quart mold. Chill firm. Serve with assorted fruits. Makes 6 to 8 servings.

With a quick recipe change, different dress-ups . . .

Now a last-minute fillip—to make a good

Colorful *trims* tempt you to taste—flavor-rich *dressing*, glistening on crisp greens, ensures you'll eat every bit!

Pineapple Dressing — Vinaigrette Dressing — Cranberry Fruit Topping — Blue-cheese Shake-up

Packaged dressing mixes — Vinegar and oil — Mayonnaise — Creamy French Dressing — Thousand Island Dressing — Clear French Dressing

salad truly distinctive!

Honey Dressing Zippy Emerald Dressing
vocado-Cheese Dressing Poppy-seed Dressing
Sour-cream Special

Garlic French Dressing Chiffonade Dressing
Red-currant Dressing Salad Dressing

Salad dressings and garnishes

Salads rely on the eye. If a salad *looks* delicious, you can depend on folks taking the first bite. But for the second, the third . . . the last forkful . . . you toss in the extra temptation of a dressing—tart, tangy or rich, spicy or sweet. The blend of *flavors* is what makes your salad disappear.

The simplest of recipes—salad dressings. Most are measure-and-mix . . . or an easy shake. Measuring can even be *pinching* if you're adventurous. Still easier, shake the packaged mixes with oil and vinegar; or start with a commercial French dressing, mayonnaise, salad dressing; add other ingredients as it suits your fancy.

Simple, yes, but nowhere do you find more subtlety of flavor. Nor will anything make you out a gourmet so fast. The exact ingredients, the expert amounts, are strictly secret till you care to flourish the information!

And besides the mystery about a dressing, the array here shows there's beauty, too. A beauty that's at its best in sparkling glass.

Look to the next few pages to inspire the very best tasting blend for tossed salads; for dressings that do justice to a lovely luncheon fruit plate, for quick variations to put some zest in the salad important to a family meal.

You've used the French dressings, salad dressing, mayonnaise. Have you specialities that start with sour cream, cream cheese? Look on pages 136 and 137. These quick dressings are delicious *on* salads or used as *dips* for crisp wedges of cucumber or lettuce, celery and carrot sticks. In these you'll find new freshness of flavor that maybe you've been missing.

Salad garnishes are on pages 138 to 143. A sprig of parsley, a sprinkle of chives, a tomato flower, cheese apples, cheese acorns. Don't miss one tantalizing trick. *Salads rely on the eye.*

Now for the very best dressings, variations . . .

First you'll find French dressings to add tantalizing flavor to your salads. Don't miss the fun of measuring (and whiffing) the almost magic ingredients.

See recipes, too, for mayonnaise, cooked dressings, toppers made with cheese and sour cream.

Final touch—salad dressings

Clear French Dressing

½ cup salad oil
2 tablespoons vinegar
2 tablespoons lemon juice
1 teaspoon sugar
½ teaspoon salt
½ teaspoon dry mustard
½ teaspoon paprika
Dash cayenne

Put all ingredients in jar; cover, and shake well before using. Makes ¾ cup.

French Mayonnaise: Rub small bowl with cut side of a clove of garlic. Slowly add two parts Clear French Dressing to one part mayonnaise, beating constantly.

Creamy French Dressing

1 teaspoon sugar
1 tablespoon paprika
1 teaspoon salt
Dash cayenne pepper
⅓ cup vinegar
1 egg
1 cup salad oil

Combine sugar and seasonings. Add vinegar and egg; beat well. Add salad oil 1 teaspoon at a time till ¼ cup has been added. Add remaining oil in gradually increasing amounts, beating well after each addition. Makes 1⅔ cups of dressing.

Tangy French Dressing

⅔ cup salad oil
⅔ cup vinegar
⅓ cup water
2 tablespoons chopped chives
  or green onion
2 teaspoons sugar
1 teaspoon paprika
2 teaspoons Worcestershire sauce
½ teaspoon salt
½ teaspoon celery salt
¼ teaspoon dry mustard
Dash pepper

Combine ingredients; shake well in covered jar. Makes 1¾ cups. Serve over greens.

Hot French Dressing

⅓ cup salad oil
2 tablespoons vinegar
2 tablespoons catsup
2 teaspoons grated onion
1 teaspoon prepared mustard
Few drops Tabasco sauce
1 teaspoon salt
¾ teaspoon chili powder
¼ teaspoon sugar
⅛ teaspoon dry mustard
Dash pepper
Dash paprika

Combine ingredients; shake well in covered jar. Makes ⅔ cup. Nice with meat salads.

Special dressing meets favorite salad—Su-perb!

What goes with what

You're the best judge of which dressing will put your salad in the delicious class. Here are guideposts . . .

Pick tangy French dressings to toss with greens, to marinate vegetables; tart or sweet ones for fruit.

Mayonnaise and salad-dressing combinations enhance meat, seafood, egg, and all molded salads.

Cooked dressing is the secret of some special potato salads. Sweet cooked dressings are luscious fruit toppings.

Cheese-flavored dressings, greens, and vegetables are natural go-togethers. Sometimes salad's simple as a lettuce wedge—dressing's the show-off.

Zippy sour-cream dressings add piquancy to fruit, vegetable salads.

Your dressing dictionary

French Dressing is a mixture of oil, vinegar, and seasonings. *Clear* French dressing separates, needs a shake every time it's served. *Creamy* French dressings are homogenized, stay mixed.

Mayonnaise is smooth, creamy—it's made by beating oil *very slowly* into seasoned vinegar and egg. (Egg emulsifies, prevents separating.) Mild flavored, it takes to extra seasonings.

Cooked Dressing has a cooked white-sauce-and-egg base, with vinegar and butter stirred in. It's fluffy, creamy, has a zippy flavor.

Salad Dressing is a rich smooth blend of mayonnaise, cooked dressing.

Seasonings to add in a jiffy

Mix your own spices and herbs into commercial dressings—go easy with curry powder, oregano, and cayenne; add more marjoram, red pepper.

Use lots of thyme, basil, rosemary, dry or fresh dill seed, celery seed.

French dressings are easy—mix seasonings, vinegar, and oil

Measure seasonings into a bowl or right into a jar. Or, use one of the packaged dressing mixes—the measuring's done for you—simply add vinegar and oil or any commercial dressing, as directed.

If you like to mix dressing right in your wooden bowl before adding greens, see how on page 52.

Add vinegar, then oil to seasonings in a jar. Try using tarragon, wine-flavored or herbed vinegars. Mix or shake *vigorously* to blend. If you have a blender, use it! When there's time, make dressing early—"aging" improves it.

Vinaigrette Dressing

1 cup clear French dressing
2 tablespoons chopped stuffed green olives
1 tablespoon chopped pimiento
1 tablespoon chopped chives
1 hard-cooked egg, chopped

Combine ingredients in jar; cover and shake vigorously until well mixed. Makes about 1¼ cups dressing. Try with salad of young spinach leaves and egg slices, or on greens.

Chiffonade Dressing

¾ cup clear French dressing
2 tablespoons chopped parsley
2 teaspoons chopped onion
1 hard-cooked egg, chopped
¼ cup chopped, cooked beets

Combine ingredients in jar; shake vigorously to blend. Makes about 1 cup dressing. Serve with bowl of tossed salad.

Chive Dressing

1 cup clear French dressing
⅓ cup dairy sour cream
1 tablespoon finely chopped chives

Combine all ingredients. Makes 1⅓ cups. Good on a citrus salad, or served with cucumbers and tomatoes.

Cottage Cheese French Dressing

1 cup creamy French dressing
3 tablespoons cottage cheese
1 tablespoon chopped sweet pickle
1 tablespoon chopped parsley

Combine all ingredients and mix well. Makes 1¼ cups. Serve over lettuce wedges, or pass with tossed vegetable salad.

Honey Orange Dressing

¾ cup clear French dressing
2 tablespoons honey
2 tablespoons orange juice
¾ teaspoon paprika

Combine ingredients in jar; cover and shake vigorously. Chill. Shake well before serving. Makes 1 cup. Serve on fruit.

Cranberry Fruit Topping

¾ cup canned jellied cranberry sauce
¾ cup salad oil
¼ cup lime or lemon juice
1 teaspoon salt

Beat cranberry sauce smooth. *Gradually* beat in oil. Blend in juice, salt. Makes 1¾ cups.

Thousand Island, French-style

½ cup salad oil
½ cup evaporated milk
¼ cup vinegar
¼ cup chili sauce or catsup
2 hard-cooked eggs, chopped
¼ cup minced green pepper
2 tablespoons minced onion
2 small cloves garlic
½ teaspoon salt
Dash pepper

Combine all ingredients in jar. Cover and shake vigorously. Chill. Remove garlic before using. Serve on greens. Makes 2 cups.

Recipes to make your reputation—easy and fun

From the left — Pineapple Dressing (page 135), Vinaigrette, and rosy Cranberry Fruit Topping

Peppy Tomato Dressing is a dieter's choice—low in calories (no oil at all!), full of flavor—from dill seed and basil, tarragon vinegar, Worcestershire, onion juice. Try it on vegetables or tossed salads.

French Pickle Sauce is fast to fix: Stir ¼ cup mustard-pickle relish into ¾ cup creamy French dressing. Serve it with a summer buffet salad-meat platter.

Tomato Soup Dressing

1 tablespoon sugar
1 teaspoon salt
1 teaspoon dry mustard
1 teaspoon paprika
1 cup salad oil
1 cup vinegar
1 can condensed tomato soup
1 tablespoon Worcestershire sauce
1 clove garlic, minced
1 small onion, chopped

Combine ingredients in jar; cover and shake thoroughly. Makes 4 cups.

Peppy Tomato Dressing

Combine one 8-ounce can seasoned tomato sauce, 2 tablespoons tarragon vinegar, 1 teaspoon onion juice, 1 teaspoon Worcestershire sauce, ½ teaspoon salt, ½ teaspoon dill seed, and ¼ teaspoon basil. Beat to blend.

Zippy Emerald Dressing

1 cup salad oil
⅓ cup salad vinegar
¼ cup chopped onion (1 small)
¼ cup minced parsley
2 tablespoons finely chopped green pepper
2 teaspoons confectioners' sugar
1½ teaspoons salt
2 teaspoons dry mustard
Dash to ½ teaspoon red pepper

Combine ingredients in jar or blender. Cover and set aside 1 hour. Shake 5 minutes or blend thoroughly. Makes about 1½ cups.

Serve with seafood, cottage cheese, or tossed green salads.

Lemon-Orange French Dressing

In jar, combine ⅓ cup sugar, 1 teaspoon salt, 1 teaspoon paprika, ¼ cup orange juice, 2½ tablespoons lemon juice, 1 tablespoon vinegar, 1 teaspoon grated onion, and 1 cup salad oil. Cover and shake vigorously to blend. Makes 1¾ cups. Try with fruits.

Glossy Fruit Dressing

½ cup sugar
1 teaspoon salt
1 teaspoon celery salt
1 teaspoon paprika
1 teaspoon dry mustard
1 teaspoon grated onion
1 cup salad oil
¼ cup vinegar

Mix dry ingredients; add onion. Add oil, a little at a time, alternately with vinegar, ending with vinegar. Beat with fork till well blended. Makes 1½ cups.

Snowy Two-way French Dressing

3 tablespoons sugar
1 teaspoon salt
1 teaspoon dry mustard
½ teaspoon white pepper
½ teaspoon onion juice
¾ cup salad oil
¼ cup white vinegar

For clear dressing: Combine ingredients in jar. Cover and shake vigorously to blend. Makes 1 cup. Nice on lettuce, tomatoes.

For creamy dressing: Mix dry ingredients; add onion juice. Add oil, a little at a time, alternately with vinegar, ending with vinegar. Beat well with fork after each addition.

Garlic flavor is for greens; honey's for fruit

Imperial House Maison Dressing

1 teaspoon golden brown prepared mustard
1 teaspoon lemon juice, fresh, frozen, or canned
1 teaspoon Worcestershire sauce
5 tablespoons olive oil
3 tablespoons chili sauce
1 tablespoon wine vinegar
1 tablespoon drained chutney, chopped
1 cup minced water cress
Salt and pepper to taste

Blend all ingredients. Pour into server and top with extra minced water cress. Serve with fruit plate. Makes 4 servings.

*To serve with seafood salad, omit chutney. Mix dressing with salad.

"Mince" garlic the easy way—squeeze it in a garlic press

Crush garlic over a wide-mouth jar or bowl. Every bit of flavor goes in dressing—and there's no garlicky aroma on board or hands. No press? Crush garlic into salt (page 52) or let half cloves stand in dressing 3 or 4 days.

Garlic French Dressing

1½ teaspoons salt
1 teaspoon sugar
½ teaspoon dry mustard
⅓ cup vinegar
1⅓ cups salad oil
5 large garlic cloves, minced

Combine ingredients in jar; cover and shake vigorously. Store several days before using. Makes 1⅔ cups.

Peppery Garlic Dressing: To above recipe, add 2 tablespoons lemon juice, dash freshly ground pepper, and, if desired, ¼ teaspoon crushed red pepper.

Hot Italian Dressing

1 teaspoon salt
1 teaspoon sugar
½ teaspoon celery salt
¼ teaspoon cayenne
¼ teaspoon dry mustard
⅓ cup vinegar
1 cup salad oil
1 clove garlic, minced
Dash Tabasco sauce

Combine ingredients in jar; cover and shake vigorously. Makes 1¼ cups.

Honey Dressing

¼ to ⅔ cup sugar
1 teaspoon dry mustard
1 teaspoon paprika
1 teaspoon celery seed
¼ teaspoon salt
⅓ cup honey
⅓ cup vinegar
1 tablespoon lemon juice
1 teaspoon grated onion
1 cup salad oil

Mix sugar, mustard, paprika, celery seed, and salt. Add honey, vinegar, lemon juice, and onion. Pour oil into mixture very slowly, beating constantly with rotary or electric beater. Makes 2 cups.

Celery-seed Dressing

½ cup sugar
1 teaspoon celery seed
1 teaspoon salt
1 teaspoon dry mustard
1 teaspoon paprika
⅓ cup lemon juice
¾ cup salad oil

Combine all ingredients except salad oil. Gradually add salad oil, beating with an electric or rotary beater until thick. Makes about 1½ cups.

Poppy-seed Dressing

½ cup sugar
Dash salt
Dash dry mustard
¼ cup salad vinegar

• • •

1 cup salad oil
½ teaspoon poppy seed

Combine sugar, salt, mustard, and vinegar; heat to boiling; cool. Add oil slowly, beating constantly with electric or rotary beater. Stir in poppy seed. Makes 1½ cups.

Neiman-Marcus Celery-seed Dressing

⅔ cup sifted confectioners' sugar
1 teaspoon dry mustard
1 teaspoon salt
3 tablespoons vinegar

• • •

1 cup salad oil
1 teaspoon paprika

• • •

1 teaspoon celery seed

Mix together sugar, mustard, salt, and vinegar. Let stand 3 hours, stirring about every 30 minutes, until of a honey consistency.

Heat one-half of the oil; to it add paprika. Strain and cool. Add paprika oil to remainder of salad oil and *beat* it slowly into first mixture.

Last, add celery seed and let stand 24 hours at room temperature. (If dressing separates, beat well before using.) Makes 1⅓ cups. This dressing is delicious on fruit salads, especially frozen ones.

Honey Quickie

Blend two parts mild-flavored honey with one part lime juice. Add dash of salt.

Nippy Nectar Dressing

1 3-ounce package cream cheese
2 tablespoons honey
1 teaspoon grated lemon peel
2 tablespoons lemon juice
½ teaspoon salt
Dash cayenne

• • •

½ cup salad oil

Soften cream cheese. Blend in remaining ingredients except salad oil. Add oil 1 tablespoon at a time, beating well after each addition. Chill. Beat again before serving over fruit salad. Makes 1 cup.

Avocado-Cheese Dressing

1 large ripe avocado
2 to 3 tablespoons lemon juice
½ cup light cream
¾ teaspoon salt
1 teaspoon prepared mustard
½ teaspoon Worcestershire sauce
¼ cup (2 ounces) sieved blue cheese

Sieve peeled avocado (makes about ¾ cup); immediately add lemon juice. Stir in remaining ingredients. Blend well. Chill. Makes 1⅓ cups. Good on shredded cabbage, lettuce wedges, fresh tomatoes.

The dressing's beautiful too!

Enjoy your prettiest bottles and bowls as servers.

You're looking in on Sour-cream Special (page 136), low bowl; and Avocado-Cheese, Honey, and Poppy-seed Dressings, tall bottles.

Super dressings made by easy additions

Mayonnaise

1 teaspoon salt
½ teaspoon dry mustard
¼ teaspoon paprika
Dash cayenne
2 egg yolks
2 tablespoons vinegar
2 cups salad oil
2 tablespoons lemon juice

Mix dry ingredients; add egg yolks and blend. Add vinegar and mix well.

Add salad oil, 1 teaspoon at a time, beating with rotary or electric beater, till ¼ cup has been added. Add remaining oil in increasing amounts, alternating last ½ cup with lemon juice. Beat in 1 tablespoon hot water to cut oil appearance. Makes 2 cups.

Thousand Island Dressing

1 cup mayonnaise
½ cup chili sauce
3 hard-cooked eggs, chopped
1½ dill pickles, chopped
⅓ cup chopped celery
1 green pepper, minced
1 small onion, minced

Combine ingredients; chill. Makes 2 cups.

Tangy Fruit Mayonnaise

Combine ½ cup mayonnaise and ½ cup sour cream. Stir in 1 tablespoon lemon juice, 1 tablespoon orange juice, and 2 teaspoons sugar. Blend till smooth. Makes 1 cup.

Lemon Mayonnaise

Combine ½ cup mayonnaise or salad dressing and ¼ cup frozen lemonade concentrate. Whip ½ cup heavy cream and fold in. Makes about 1½ cups dressing.

Blue Cheese Mayonnaise

Press 2 tablespoons crumbled blue cheese through fine sieve. Mix with ½ cup mayonnaise, 4 teaspoons milk, and a few drops of Tabasco sauce. Makes about ⅔ cup.

Creamy Horseradish Dressing

1 cup mayonnaise or salad dressing
½ cup heavy cream, whipped
¼ cup prepared horseradish, drained
2 teaspoons sugar
¾ teaspoon salt
Dash cayenne
4 drops Tabasco sauce
3 drops Worcestershire sauce

Measure mayonnaise into bowl; fold in remaining ingredients. Chill. Makes about 1⅔ cups. Nice with meat, seafood salads.

Chili Mayonnaise Topper

Slowly stir ½ cup chili sauce into ½ cup mayonnaise. Add ½ cup creamy French dressing and 1 teaspoon Worcestershire sauce. Mix well. Makes about 1½ cups.

Creamy Mayonnaise

Whip ½ cup heavy cream; fold into 1 cup mayonnaise until well blended. Makes about 2 cups dressing. Serve with fruit.

Honey Mayonnaise

Combine ½ cup mayonnaise, ¼ cup honey, ½ teaspoon celery seed, ¼ teaspoon paprika, and 1 tablespoon lemon juice. Blend well. Makes about ⅔ cup.

Fluffy Cucumber Dressing

1 cup heavy cream, whipped
½ teaspoon salt
¼ teaspoon paprika
2 to 3 tablespoons lemon juice
¼ cup mayonnaise or salad dressing
1 cup pared finely chopped cucumber, drained

Combine whipped cream, salt, and paprika. Gradually fold in lemon juice. Add mayonnaise and cucumber. Serve at once. Makes 2½ cups.

To match picture on page 79, serve in cucumber boat; top with pineapple tidbits.

Red-currant Dressing

1 cup currant jelly
½ cup mayonnaise
½ cup heavy cream, whipped

With rotary beater, beat currant jelly till soft and smooth. Blend in mayonnaise. Fold in whipped cream. Makes about 2 cups.

Cooked Dressing

2 tablespoons enriched flour
2 tablespoons sugar
1 teaspoon salt
1 teaspoon dry mustard
Few grains cayenne
2 slightly beaten egg yolks or
1 beaten egg
¾ cup milk
¼ cup vinegar
1½ teaspoons butter or margarine

Mix dry ingredients; add egg and milk; cook in double boiler over hot, *not boiling*, water till thick, stirring constantly. Add vinegar and butter; mix well. Cool. Makes 1 cup.

Pineapple Dressing

⅓ cup sugar
4 teaspoons cornstarch
¼ teaspoon salt
1 cup unsweetened pineapple juice
¼ cup orange juice
3 tablespoons lemon juice
2 beaten eggs
2 3-ounce packages cream cheese

Combine dry ingredients in saucepan; blend in fruit juices. Cook, stirring constantly, till clear, about 5 to 8 minutes. Slowly stir into eggs. Return to saucepan and cook over low heat, stirring constantly, 3 to 5 minutes, or till mixture thickens slightly. Cool 5 minutes. Soften cream cheese; beat cooled mixture into it. Chill. Makes 2 cups.

Lemonade Dressing

2 eggs
⅓ cup sugar
1 6-ounce can lemonade concentrate
1 cup heavy cream, whipped

Beat eggs in top of double boiler; stir in sugar and lemonade concentrate. Cook and stir over simmering water till thick. Cool thoroughly. Fold in whipped cream. Chill. Makes 3 cups. Serve with fruit salad.

Fruit Salad Topper

½ cup sugar
1 tablespoon paprika
1½ teaspoons enriched flour
1 teaspoon dry mustard
½ cup vinegar
1 tablespoon lemon juice
1 cup salad oil
1 tablespoon onion juice
1 tablespoon celery seed

Sift together dry ingredients. Add vinegar. Cook over low heat stirring constantly, till slightly thick. Add lemon juice; cool to room temperature. Add oil in slow stream, beating with electric beater. Beat in onion juice; add celery seed. Makes 1½ cups. Stir before use.

Russian Dressing

¼ cup sugar
3 tablespoons water
1½ teaspoons celery seed
½ teaspoon salt
½ teaspoon paprika
2½ tablespoons lemon juice
1 tablespoon Worcestershire sauce
1 tablespoon vinegar
1 cup salad oil
½ cup catsup
¼ cup grated onion

Cook sugar and water till mixture spins a thread (232°). Cool. Combine remaining ingredients; beat in syrup. Chill. Makes 2 cups.

You can buy or make these 3 dressings

Bowl holds Mayonnaise; bottle, Creamy French. Under lid is Thousand Island.

They're wonderful dips or easy toppings

Horseradish Sauce

1 cup dairy sour cream
½ to 1 tablespoon prepared horseradish
½ teaspoon salt
1 tablespoon grated onion
½ teaspoon paprika

Combine ingredients; blend well. Sprinkle with additional paprika. Makes about 1 cup.

Spring Garden Dip

1 cup dairy sour cream
½ cup mayonnaise
1 tablespoon sugar
1 teaspoon salt
Dash pepper
¼ cup minced green onions
¼ cup minced radishes
¼ cup minced cucumber, drained
¼ cup minced green pepper
1 clove garlic, minced

Blend sour cream, mayonnaise, sugar, salt, and pepper. Stir in minced vegetables. Serve in bowl; border with additional minced vegetables, if desired (see page 50). Pass carrot sticks to dip. Makes 2 cups.

Sour Cream Special

1 cup dairy sour cream
½ cup finely chopped, well-drained cucumber
¼ cup finely chopped green onions
¼ cup finely chopped radishes
1 tablespoon tarragon vinegar
1 to 1½ teaspoons prepared horseradish
¾ teaspoon salt

Combine ingredients; chill. Makes about 1⅓ cups. Use as a dip for crisp cucumber and celery sticks, a dressing for lettuce wedges. Top with extra radish, if desired.

Sweet Sour-cream Dressing

Combine 1 cup dairy sour cream with 2 tablespoons white vinegar. Add 1 to 2 tablespoons sugar and ½ teaspoon salt. Toss with crisp shredded cabbage. Or serve over tomatoes, cucumbers, or fruit salad.

Strawberry-Sour Cream Sauce

Add ½ teaspoon salt to 1 cup dairy sour cream. Fold in ¼ cup frozen strawberries. Makes about 1¼ cups. Serve over fruits.

This will keep 'em nibbling their "vitamins"

The dip is Sour Cream Special—finely chopped cucumber, green onion, radishes; sour cream; a little salt and vinegar; as much horseradish as you dare. What's easier?

Fall to, everybody. You can dip in a stick of celery, cucumber, carrot curl. Or slide a lettuce wedge and slice of tomato onto your plate, spoon dressing over.

Chived Sour Cream, cucumber, tomatoes—*there's* a delicious salad for you. And it's this easy: Blend 1 cup dairy sour cream, ½ cup mayonnaise. Stir in ¼ cup snipped chives, 2 tablespoons tarragon vinegar, ½ teaspoon salt, and dash pepper.

Caraway-Cheese Dressing will make this salad sing. Mix ⅔ cup salad dressing, 3 tablespoons light cream, 1 teaspoon caraway or dill seed, ¼ cup finely slivered, sharp American cheese.

Ripe Olive-Sour Cream Dressing

1 cup dairy sour cream
1 cup finely chopped ripe olives
2 teaspoons sugar
2 teaspoons lemon juice
¼ teaspoon celery salt
Dash salt

Combine all ingredients. Chill. Serve with crisp fresh vegetables. (See page 67.)

Roquefort Dressing

Blend 1 part softened cream cheese with 2 parts softened Roquefort cheese. Add French dressing till consistency you prefer.

Blue-cheese Chef's Dressing

3 ounces blue cheese, crumbled
(about ¾ cup)
2 tablespoons vinegar
1 teaspoon anchovy paste
Dash steak sauce
1 tablespoon lemon juice
½ cup olive oil
½ clove garlic, minced
Salt and pepper

Combine ingredients thoroughly. Makes 1 cup. Serve with Chef's and green salads.

Blue-cheese Shake-up

1 ounce blue cheese, crumbled
(about ¼ cup)
½ teaspoon salt
½ teaspoon dry mustard
½ teaspoon paprika
Dash cayenne
½ cup salad oil
3 tablespoons salad vinegar

Combine ingredients in jar; cover and shake well. Makes ¾ cup. (See picture, page 126.) Toss with green salads.

Blue-cheese Dip

1 8-ounce package cream cheese
4 ounces blue cheese, crumbled
(about 1 cup)
¼ cup evaporated milk
3 tablespoons chopped pimiento
⅓ cup chopped green pepper
¼ teaspoon garlic salt

Soften cream cheese; add blue cheese; beat till creamy. Stir in remaining ingredients. Chill the dip until ½ hour before serving. Sprinkle with paprika, if desired. Serve with crisp celery and carrot sticks, crackers. Makes about 2 cups.

Picture-pretty garnishes

The garnish is the eyecatcher, the come-on-and-eat-me, the *fun* of salad-making. It can be as simple as a saucy parsley sprig or as elaborate as our seashell ring below. Simple *or* elaborate, it rewards you with its beauty and all the raves it wins. Look here for ideas to set your company talking, and for "talking" your family into eating!

Apples—Dip bright-skinned wedges or rings in lemon juice; arrange on Waldorf.

Coconut—Sprinkle over fruit.

Cherries—Make bouquets of stems-on fresh or maraschino cherries with mint.

Cream Cheese—Roll balls in nutmeats, group on water cress, for fruit salads.

Greens—Tuck under; use sprigs atop.

Nuts—Sprinkle over dressing, on fruit.

Olives—Arrange slices or whole olives.

Pineapple Slices—Unmold individual salads on them; snip, twist for platter trim.

Strawberries—Group on greens, halved, or whole with stems on.

Seashell Ice Ring keeps buffet salad cool as a breeze from the sea; tiny shells add to the nautical air.

Star-bright, this delectable garnish for aspic or fruit salad ring

Dust cooky sheet with confectioners' sugar. On it, spread softened cream cheese (¼ inch deep); chill. Cut stars with cooky cutter dipped in confectioners' sugar.

Arrange stars in bottom of oiled mold. Add gelatin mixture to level of stars; chill firm. Add remaining gelatin; chill firm.

Before unmolding, loosen edges with knife. Wrap wet, warm cloth around mold a second, place platter over salad, invert.

Salad looks a little "plainjane"? Needs some greens, a quickie trim

Seashell Ice Ring

Fill a large ring mold (12 to 15½ inches in diameter) about one-fourth to one-third full of water. Arrange seashells in water. (Be sure the shells are completely covered with water so they will stay in place.)

Freeze. Fill remainder of mold with water and again freeze firm. One hour before ice ring is to be used, remove it from mold and allow enough to melt to show shells better.

We show tomato aspic served in center, and border of shrimp and water cress.

Note: It's a good idea to use a rack on your serving tray so food won't be in water as the ice melts. Cover rack with greens.

Trim Ideas for Molded Salads

For ring molds: Center with bowlful of dressing; bouquet of greens laced with shrimp; mound of mixed melon balls or other fruits.

For loaf molds: Down center overlap slices of egg, cucumber, tomato, or pickle; line up cutouts of jellied cranberry sauce or pimiento. Or fix a "flower" as shown on page 92.

Pimiento crescents quickly dress up a tuna- or salmon-salad mold. With small, round cutter, make a half-circle cut in piece of pimiento; move cutter up about ½ inch from first cut; press again. Cut several crescents this way.

Line up the crescents with stuffed-olive slices down center of mold. Other times, cut out pimiento stars, diamonds, strips.

Just a touch fancy to add to the fun of eating

With a can of fruit and a package of gelatin you're ready to make these trims

Pineapple rings are a quick trim you can keep on hand. Here they're halved, arranged as a border. In centers are halved Tokay grapes. Another quickie with pineapple or apple rings—split one ring, slip it through center of another to make figure 8; add sprigs of greens.

Chill bright gelatin (red here) till firm, in a rectangular baking dish; then cut individual salads with a cooky cutter (we used a heart). Slide heart onto pineapple slice on lettuce ruffle. The extra gelatin, cubed, comes in handy for dessert or makes pretty cottage cheese trim.

Tiny Cheese Apples or Cheese Acorns are for "munching" with fruit salads

Cheese Apples: Moisten shredded cheese with mayonnaise. Roll in balls. Dent each end; stick whole clove in one end, half a green toothpick in other. Roll in paprika for rosy "cheeks," as shown.

Cheese Acorns: Make balls from chunk of cheese with melon-ball cutter. With doughnut-hole cutter, cut tiny circles from cheese slice; dip in nutmeg. Peg a circle to each ball with a whole clove "stem."

Garnishes this good to eat can be the whole salad or the beautiful trim. Take it easy—they're simple, speedy to fix

Pipe a neat frill of softened cream cheese on plump prunes or, quicker still, spoon it on in a fluff. Serve on gay orange slices, or pineapple, or juicy peach halves. Or top each prune with a big perfect walnut for fruit-plate trim.

Jellied-cranberry-sauce cutouts are a fast and festive touch for fruit, chicken, or turkey salads. Use cooky cutter. Or make your own pattern to cut around. Note new twist with pineapple—garnish for fruit-salad bowl, platter. One slice, snipped, curls into center of another. →

Hard-cook a few eggs to make a trim that's bound to be talked about

Rainbow-colored eggs make ham platter extra-special. Color eggs with summer-drink powder (page 119); turn some into Deviled Egg "daisies" (page 118); pipe cream cheese on others.

← "Flower" with petals of hard-cooked egg and golden yolk center makes chicken salad look all the more scrumptious. Pimiento strips, parsley, French endive are "finishing touches."

Bright vegetables make snappy trims

Zip with the knife, snip with the scissors. What do you know—a tomato, a pickle, even a turnip can be so glamorous!

Turnip Lilies trim the meat platter or relish tray. For each lily, cut two *thin* turnip slices; curve to shape flower. Slip in the carrot-stick center. Anchor with toothpicks. Crisp in ice water.

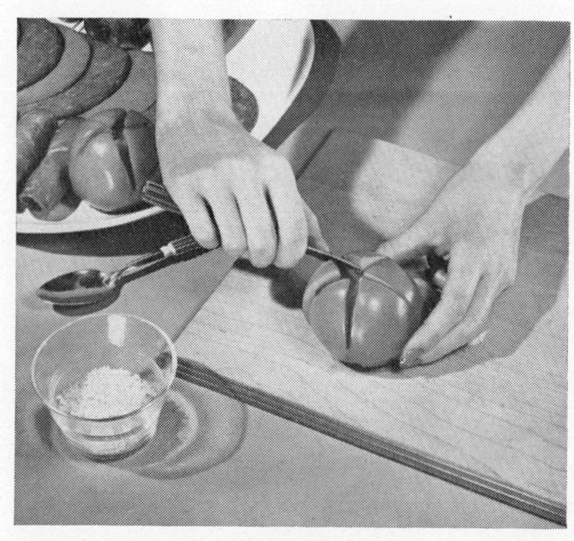

Tomato Roses trim a luncheon meat platter. *One* tops off a beautiful bowl of tossed salad. *One* on a ruffle of lettuce makes an individual salad.

Turn tomato stem end down. Cut five or six petals — cut through skin but not into seed pockets. Gently separate petals from tomato. Sprinkle with sieved, hard-cooked egg yolks for a golden center.

Snippets of chives dress up a tomato and cottage-cheese salad, or a bowlful of dressing—add peppy flavor, too.

Do the snipping on waxed paper, then you're ready to shake the chives onto the salad or dressing this neat and easy way. When you want minced parsley get out your scissors, too.

Ripe-olive and carrot tricks

Topper on coleslaw is chain of ripe olive slices. Cut three slices from pitted olive. Snip one slice to join other two "links."

Slim carrot sticks are poked through pitted olives to make colorful bundles.

Pick a piquant pickle for a very pretty trim! How to slice, fan, or fill it . . .

For Pickle Accordions, cut off ends; then slice crosswise, almost but not quite through. Bend pickle gently so slices separate at top.

Make Pickle Fans by slicing pickle lengthwise almost to stem end, making thin slices. Spread each fan as shown and press uncut end so fan will hold its shape. Nice with meat salads.

Start Stuffed-pickle Slices by cutting thin slice from stem end of large dill. Hollow pickle with apple corer. Stuff with softened cream cheese or any spreading cheese. Chill well; slice.

Frosted Grapes in a bunch—cool, sugary—garnish chicken, fruit salads

Jellied Chicken Almond (see page 111) rates a parade of trims for a beautiful salad luncheon. To "frost" the grapes, brush with slightly beaten egg white or with fruit juice. Sprinkle with sugar. Let dry on a rack before arranging on plate or platter.

Other trims on luncheon plate—cucumber sticks (leave peel on), their edges dipped in bright paprika; glossy ripe olives; Pickle Fans (see how-to in picture above).

For the tiny tomato roses shown here, you simply cut an X in top, spread tomato open. Season; add a dab of mayonnaise and a sprinkle of sieved, hard-cooked egg yolk.

What's for dessert? Fresh-baked, lushly frosted layer cake; plenty of hot coffee.

Relish-tray treats

To make an accordion of a cucumber, slice almost through, slip radish slices in cuts.

Crisp cauliflowerets have parsley topknot. Melon balls are nestled in water cress. For Carrot Zigzags, see page 71. Dip is French Mayonnaise.

What-to-eat with your

puzzler? Salad meals and salad partners

If meal monotony is one of your problems, you can stop here. You'll find supper and luncheon plans with salad the mainstay . . . hearty dinners with salad the light touch . . . meals where salad doubles for dessert or comes to the table as an appetizer.

It's handy to have a meal in mind when it's your turn to ask the girls over or when Dad wants to know what to serve at a stag. There are ideas aplenty in this chapter. We have planned guest buffets (the casual type everyone likes) . . . family suppers and back-yard picnics . . . Lenten and Friday specials . . . holiday feasts . . . keep-out-of-the-kitchen cool-offs . . . summer meals so refreshing the heat is forgotten!

In leafing through your Salad Book, when you come to a recipe that intrigues you, turn to these pages to see what you might like to serve with it. Use these meal plans to spark an idea. Some you may want to "borrow for keeps" just as is; others you'll want to personalize to suit yourself. There's good variation here to keep your family happy—and you, too!

A cool salad calls for an oven-hot bread as a partner

Notice how we always add something *hot* to a *cold* supper or luncheon. The whole meal will taste better that way, be better for you. Perhaps we start off with a cup of steaming soup or end with freshly brewed coffee or tea. *And* more than likely there'll be a tempting surprise in the bread basket —*hot* muffins, rolls, crackers, or other crisps. Because these are such natural salad partners, they rate their own recipe section.

Too busy to fuss? Zip open a box of muffin or biscuit mix, or a tube of refrigerated biscuits. Fix-ups for these packaged helpers are quick and good. Don't miss Bacon Twists (page 155) or Snacko (page 153)!

Some salads almost demand a bread as robust as Garlic-butter Slices (page 155); others need a dainty kind like Blueberry Muffins (page 150). Take a whirl through the chapter to get acquainted with all the choices.

How refreshing and delicious a salad meal can be!

← The salad's Cucumber Ring (page 87). The cool, good eating with it, on basket tray—fresh greens and green onions, wedges of tomato, pink shrimp.

For the shrimp—lemon cuts tipped with bright paprika, Horse-radish Sauce (page 136) in bowl. Crisp Caraway Logs (page 155) and corn sticks are in triple pottery server; lift the lid for a butter ball. Dessert for leisurely nibbling with hot coffee—cookies, California walnuts, gumdrop confections.

Tossed green salad is a "must" in Italian meals Choose greens to suit your fancy—here crisp lettuce and escarole glisten with garlic dressing. Main dish is lasagne—could be pizza. Dessert? Spumone (Italian-style ice cream).

For inspiration—salad meal plans

Lunches, suppers with salad the main dish

On a Summer Evening

Hot Humpty-dumpty Salad in Bread Boat*
Buttered Corn
Radish Dominoes* Ripe Olives
Fudge Cupcakes
Hot Coffee

It's a Man's Party

Consomme on Ice
Corned-beef Salad Mold*
Perfect Potato Salad*
Cabbage-patch Coleslaw*
Buttered Rye Bread Dill-pickle Sticks
Chilled Watermelon
Iced Tea

Fruit Salad Luncheon

Red-and-white Fruit Mold*
Red-currant Dressing*
Frosted Grapes* Banana Cuts*
Tea Muffins* Hot Coffee

Lazy-day Back-yard Supper

Ham Loaf*
Deviled Eggs* Easy Aspic*
Hot French Bread Celery Fans*
Cantaloupe Sundaes Iced Tea

Chef's Patio Picnic

Hot Tomato Bouillon
Chef's Bowl*
Garlic-butter Slices*
Strawberry Shortcake Hot Coffee

**For recipes, see index*

Bridge-party Salad Luncheon

Crab-Meat Tomato Accordions*
Shoestring Potatoes or Potato Chips
Cheese Straws*
Olives, Pickles
Honeydew and Cantaloupe Slices
Tall Glasses of Lemonade

Lenten Luncheon

Tuna Salad (Basic Seafood*)
Herbed Potato Chips*
Buttered Peas With Mushrooms
Stuffed Green Olives Sweet-pickle Chips
Slim-Jim Bread Sticks*
Baked Custard Sugar Wafers
Hot Coffee

For the Girls

Chicken Salad in Raspberry Ring*
Asparagus Spears with Lemon Butter
Bran Muffins* Stuffed Celery Sticks*
Lemon Chiffon Pie
Salted Nuts Hot Coffee

Garden-wheel Buffet

Tart French dressing adds tangy flavor to cooked peas, green beans, baby Limas, and cauliflower. Let guests help themselves!

Madrilene in Honeydew Cups*
Supper Salad Wheel*
Bacon Cornettes*
Peach Lattice Pie Iced Tea or Hot Coffee

Friday-night Supper

Chilled Tomato Juice
Macaroni-and-Cheese Salad in Pepper Cups*
Hard-cooked Egg Wedges Celery Sticks
Crisp Caraway Logs*
Chilled Peaches Crisp Cookies
Hot Coffee

After the Game

Hot Vegetable-juice Cocktail
Casserole Ham Salad*
Buttered Green Beans Julienne
Sweet Apple Ring*
Brown-and-serve Rolls
Mince Tarts with Cheese Wedges
Hot Coffee or Mugs of Cold Milk

Thanksgivingtime Buffet

Mugs of Hot Tomato Soup
Turkey-Green Grape Salad*
Cranberry Cups*
Sesame Wedges*
Pumpkin Ice-cream Pie
Hot Coffee

Home-for-the-holidays

Chicken-Cranberry Layers*
Buttered Broccoli
Radish Roses* Carrot Curls*
Hot Parker House Rolls Butter Balls
Noel Eggnog Pie Hot Coffee

**For recipes, see index*

←
A hearty ham salad men go for

Skillet Ham-Potato Salad* is an old-time hot salad with zesty cheese flavor. You get a fast start with canned ham. Nice to serve — bacon-wrapped franks, relishes, and hard rolls.

Dinners that feature the "go-with-meat" salads

July Smorgasbord

A recipe for simple entertaining! Fix salad and cucumbers ahead. Arrange meat, cheese on platter —each guest makes his own sandwich—

Assorted Cold Cuts and Cheeses
Old-time Kidney-bean Salad*
Tomato Slices — Dutch Cucumbers*
Buttered Rye Bread
Orange Sherbet — Hot Coffee

**For recipes, see index*

Summer Supper on the Terrace

Fried Chicken
Potato-salad Mold*
Baked Beans
Hot Boston Brown Bread
Watermelon Circles — Iced Tea

Easy-on-the-hostess Buffet

Baked Ham
Candied Sweet Potatoes
Buttered Green Beans
Golden Apricot Molds*
Sweet Sour-cream Dressing*
Hot Biscuits With Butter
Angel Cake With Cherry Sauce
Hot Coffee

Offer hot breads and crisps as salad

Nowadays "fancy" muffins fairly jump from the box! Choose from muffin quartet on Lazy Susan—all made from packaged mixes.

Stacked between preserves are orange muffins; left of cherries are raisin-bran, corn, date muffins.

Just open a package for these muffins

Sunday Dinner Special

Fruit Cup*
Roast Beef
Parsleyed Potatoes   Buttered Peas
Tossed Green Salad*
Clear French Dressing*
Hot Rolls
Warm Apple Pie   Hot Coffee

Fall Feast

Chilled Cranberry-juice Cocktail
Braised Pork Chops
Baked Squash   Creamed Onions
Pear-Waldorf with Swiss Cheese*
Brown-and-serve Rolls
Warm Gingerbread
Hot Coffee

Supper and snack specials that star dessert salads

Salad Tops It Off!

French-fried Shrimp   Chili Hot Sauce*
Hot Potato Chips   Buttered Asparagus
Celery Sticks   Radish Accordions*
Cloverleaf Rolls
Twenty-four Hour Salad*   Hot Coffee

After-the-theater Coffeetime

Strawberry-Pineapple Cups*
Fancy Cookies   Hot Coffee   Salted Nuts
*For recipes, see index

partners that give a lilt to the meal

Banana-Date Loaf

¾ cup mashed fully ripe banana
⅓ cup water
1 package date-muffin mix

Combine banana and water. Prepare batter from muffin mix by package directions, *using banana mixture in place of the water*.

Pour into greased 8½x4½x2½-inch loaf pan. Bake in moderate oven (350°) 45 to 55 minutes, till done. Remove from pan; cool.

Teatime Slices

Prepare batter from 1 package of orange-muffin mix, according to package directions. Fold in ¾ cup canned whole cranberry sauce and 1 cup chopped California walnuts.

Spoon into 6 greased 6-ounce frozen-juice-concentrate cans. Bake in moderate oven (375°) 30 to 35 minutes, or till done.

Cool about 5 minutes, then ease out of cans with spatula (cut end out of can if necessary). For easy slicing, wait a day.

Muffin mix gives head start on brand new recipes. At left is Banana-Date Loaf — from a date-muffin mix. Or add cranberry sauce and walnuts to orange-muffin mix for Teatime Slices. Bake in frozen-juice-concentrate cans for rounds.

Easy nut breads with muffin mixes

Serve them fresh-baked, fragrant—with lots of butter

Tea Muffins

⅓ cup shortening
⅓ cup sugar
½ teaspoon vanilla
• • •
1 egg
• • •
1¾ cups sifted enriched flour
2 teaspoons baking powder
½ teaspoon salt
⅔ cup milk
• • •
Orange marmalade or currant jelly (optional)

Cream together the shortening, sugar, and vanilla till light and fluffy. Add the egg and beat well. Sift together the dry ingredients. Add to creamed mixture alternately with milk, mixing just to blend.

Drop batter from spoon into greased muffin pans, filling ⅔ full. If desired, top each muffin with a teaspoon of orange marmalade or currant jelly. Bake in hot oven (400°) about 20 minutes or till done.

Serve a basketful of warm Tea Muffins with summer fresh fruit plates.

Bacon Cornettes

10 to 12 slices bacon, diced
• • •
1 cup sifted enriched flour
¼ cup sugar
4 teaspoons baking powder
¾ teaspoon salt
1 cup yellow corn meal
• • •
2 eggs
1 cup milk
¼ cup salad oil or soft shortening

Cook bacon till crisp; drain. Sift together flour, sugar, baking powder, and salt; stir in corn meal. Add eggs, milk, and salad oil.

With rotary or electric beater, beat till just smooth, about 1 minute (do not overbeat). Stir in bacon bits.

Drop batter from spoon into greased muffin pans, filling ⅔ full. If desired, top with a few bits of uncooked bacon. Bake in hot oven (425°) 20 to 25 minutes.

Makes about 1 dozen muffins.

Date Muffins

1¾ cups sifted enriched flour
2 tablespoons sugar
2½ teaspoons baking powder
¾ teaspoon salt
• • •
⅔ cup coarsely cut pitted dates
• • •
1 well-beaten egg
¾ cup milk
⅓ cup salad oil or melted shortening

Sift together flour, sugar, baking powder, and salt into mixing bowl; stir in chopped dates. Make a well in the center.

Combine egg, milk, and salad oil; add all at once to dry ingredients. Stir quickly only till dry ingredients are moistened.

Drop batter from spoon into greased muffin pans, filling ⅔ full. Bake in a hot oven (400°) about 25 minutes. Makes 1 dozen.

Extra good with fruit or cheese salads.

Blueberry Muffins

1¾ cups sifted enriched flour
¼ cup sugar
2½ teaspoons baking powder
¾ teaspoon salt
• • •
1 well-beaten egg
¾ cup milk
⅓ cup shortening, melted
• • •
1 cup fresh or well-drained frozen blueberries

Sift together the flour, sugar, baking powder, and salt into a mixing bowl. Make a well in the center.

Combine egg, milk, and shortening; add all at once to dry ingredients. Stir quickly only till dry ingredients are moistened.

Gently stir blueberries into batter. Drop batter into greased muffin pans, filling ⅔ full.

If desired, sprinkle tops with a little sugar. Bake in hot oven (400°) 20 to 25 minutes. Makes 1 dozen.

Oven-hot Blueberry Muffins are good with all salads—see picture, page 94.

Count on little hot breads to dress up a salad meal

In the blue cozy—Orange Spirals, tender and gooey raised rolls to accent a fruit salad (see recipe on page 155). At top are Bacon Cornettes—golden muffins to go with green salads; left, crusty Popovers—top flavormates with any salad.

Bran Muffins

- 2 tablespoons shortening
- 3 tablespoons sugar
- 1 egg

• • •

- ¾ cup milk
- 1 cup branflakes

• • •

- 1 cup sifted enriched flour
- 2 teaspoons baking powder
- ½ teaspoon salt

Cream together the shortening and sugar till light and fluffy. Add the egg and beat well. Stir in milk; add the bran and mix well.

Sift together the flour, baking powder, and salt; add to bran mixture and stir just till dry ingredients are moistened.

Drop the batter from a spoon into greased muffin pans, filling ⅔ full. Bake in hot oven (425°) 20 to 25 minutes or till muffins are a golden brown. Makes 1 dozen.

Bran Muffins accent the flavor and crispness of vegetable salads. On the cover, they are heaped in a basket with Tea Muffins.

Popovers

- 2 eggs
- 1 cup milk
- 1 cup sifted enriched flour
- ½ teaspoon salt

• • •

- 1 tablespoon salad oil or melted shortening

Place the eggs in a mixing bowl; add milk, flour, and salt. Beat 1½ minutes with rotary or electric beater. Add salad oil; beat ½ minute. (Do not overbeat.)

Fill 6 to 8 *well-greased* custard cups ½ full. Bake in a very hot oven (475°) 15 minutes. Reduce heat to moderate (350°); continue baking about 25 to 30 minutes, until popovers are browned and firm.

A few minutes before removing from oven, prick each popover with a fork to allow the steam to escape. If you like your popovers dry inside, turn off the oven and then leave in 30 minutes with door ajar. Serve popovers hot with plenty of butter.

Makes 6 to 8 popovers.

Butter-Pecan Bread

2¼ cups sifted enriched flour
2 teaspoons baking powder
½ teaspoon soda
½ teaspoon salt
½ teaspoon cinnamon
¼ teaspoon nutmeg

• • •

1 cup brown sugar
1 cup chopped pecans

• • •

1 slightly beaten egg
1 cup buttermilk
2 tablespoons butter or margarine, melted

Sift together the flour, baking powder, soda, salt, and spices; stir in sugar and pecans. Combine egg, buttermilk, and butter; add to dry ingredients, stirring just until moistened. Pour into greased 9½x5x3-inch loaf pan. Bake in moderate oven (350°) 45 minutes or till done. Cool slightly before removing from the pan.

Sandwich thin slices of Butter-Pecan Bread with softened cream cheese and orange marmalade. Serve with fruit salad.

Orange Nut Bread

Peel from 2 large oranges*

• • •

2¼ cups sifted enriched flour
¾ cup sugar
3 teaspoons baking powder
1 teaspoon salt
1 cup chopped California walnuts

• • •

2 beaten eggs
1 cup milk
3 tablespoons butter, melted

Prepare orange peel first: With sharp knife, on cutting board, cut peel in thin strips, then lay several strips together and chop fine. (You'll need 1 cup of chopped peel.)

Sift together the flour, sugar, baking powder, and salt; add orange peel and walnuts. Combine the eggs, milk, and melted butter; add all at once to the dry ingredients, stirring just till flour is moistened.

Pour into greased 9½x5½x3-inch loaf pan. Bake in a moderate oven (350°) about 55 minutes or till done. Remove bread from pan and cool on wire rack.

*Use orange sections in salad.

Cheese Fold-overs—so fancy you'd think they were a bake-shop specialty! But *you* make them in jig time with a stick of packaged pastry mix, sharp cheese, a sprinkle of poppy seed. Flip dough over, as shown above, or pinch up two opposite corners for "baskets."

Cheese Straws—rich pastry made doubly good with sharp American and Parmesan cheeses. The pretty grooved pattern is made with a cooky press. Remember these pastries to go with tossed green salads or fruit cups. Or serve with a tomato-juice appetizer.

Waffled Orange Nut Bread

Slice Orange Nut Bread in ½-inch slices. Place the slices (*not* buttered) in hot waffle iron and toast until the bread is browned in waffled pattern. Serve hot.

Sesame Wedges

1 1-pound unsliced sandwich loaf
¼ cup softened butter
¼ cup sharp spreading cheese
Few drops Tabasco sauce
¼ cup sesame seed, toasted

Trim top and side crusts from loaf. Place loaf on ungreased baking sheet and cut zigzag in 7 to 8 wedges, *almost to bottom crust* (see picture on page 65). Blend butter, cheese, and Tabasco sauce. Spread between wedges and over top and sides of loaf. Tie string around loaf to hold together; press sesame seed onto top and sides. Bake in moderate oven (350°) about 20 minutes.

Slim-Jim Bread Sticks

Prepare 1 package hot-roll mix according to package directions. When time to shape, place dough on lightly floured surface. Turn several times. Cut off piece slightly smaller than golf ball. Roll to get 10- to 12-inch stick. Place on greased cooky sheet.

Brush with mixture of 1 slightly beaten egg white and 1 tablespoon water. Let rise uncovered about 20 minutes.

Brush rolls again with egg-white mixture. Sprinkle with coarse salt. Bake in very hot oven (450°) about 12 minutes. Makes about 2½ dozen sticks.

Snacko

1 8-ounce package corn-muffin mix
1 cup coarsely chopped salted peanuts
½ cup grated Parmesan cheese
1 teaspoon garlic salt
3 tablespoons butter, melted

Prepare corn-muffin mix according to package directions; spread evenly in a well-greased 15½x10½x1-inch jelly-roll pan. Sprinkle with peanuts, cheese, and garlic salt; drizzle butter over top. Bake in moderate oven (375°) about 25 minutes or till crisp and lightly browned. Immediately cut in squares or break in pieces; cool slightly and remove from pan.

Cheese Straws

½ cup shortening
1 cup shredded sharp process American cheese
3 tablespoons grated Parmesan cheese
1 cup sifted enriched flour
¾ teaspoon salt

Cream shortening; add cheeses and beat well. Sift together flour and salt; stir into the creamed mixture. Mix to smooth dough. Force through ¾- to 1-inch-wide saw-tooth flat attachment of cooky press. Press out in 5-inch lengths on ungreased cooky sheet.

Bake in moderate oven (350°) about 12 minutes. Let cool on sheet a few minutes; then remove carefully. Makes 2½ dozen.

Cheese Fold-overs

1 packaged pastry-mix stick
½ cup shredded sharp process American cheese
2 tablespoons cold water
• • •
Melted butter or margarine
Poppy seed

Crumble pastry stick and mix with cheese. Sprinkle water over, one tablespoon at a time, mixing well with fork till dough forms a ball. On lightly floured surface, roll very thin in a 12x10-inch rectangle (less than ⅛ inch thick).

Cut in 2-inch squares; brush with butter and sprinkle with poppy seed. Fold each square over in a triangle; brush with more butter and sprinkle with more seed; seal edges. Bake on ungreased cooky sheet in very hot oven (450°) about 8 minutes or till lightly browned. Makes 3 dozen.

Coney Sticks

6 coney rolls
¼ cup garlic spread
¼ cup butter or margarine
¼ cup grated Parmesan cheese
Poppy seed or sesame seed

Cut rolls in fourths lengthwise to make "fingers." Melt garlic spread and butter; brush on cut sides of rolls. Sprinkle with grated cheese and poppy seed.

Place on cooky sheet and bake in very hot oven (450°) 5 to 8 minutes or till toasty. Serve hot. Makes 24 sticks.

It's almost pizza!

Calico Cheese Cuts are thin and crusty, with a baked-on cheese-pimiento topping that's full of zesty flavor.

They're just right with a crisp tossed salad. Snip in servings with scissors.

At left we're pressing the rolled dough into a jelly-roll pan. After rising, the dough gets cheese topper before going in oven.

Calico Cheese Cuts

1 package hot-roll mix
2 eggs
⅔ cup evaporated milk or light cream
1 teaspoon salt
1 teaspoon celery seed
¼ cup chopped pimiento
4 cups shredded sharp process cheese
¼ teaspoon coarse black pepper

Prepare dough and let rise as directed on mix package. Beat eggs with milk just to blend. Add salt, celery seed, pimiento, and cheese. Divide dough in half. On lightly floured surface roll to a little less than ¼ inch. Pat out each piece very thin in a well-greased 15½x10½x1-inch jelly-roll pan. Let rise till light (30 to 60 minutes). Spread the topping evenly on dough, almost to edge. Sprinkle with pepper. Bake in hot oven (425°) about 12 minutes. Snip in 4x2-inch rectangles. Makes about 32. Serve hot.

Offer crusty garlic loaf or biscuits with greens, sweet rolls with fruit

Orange Spirals

1 package active dry yeast or 1 cake compressed yeast
¼ cup water
1 cup milk, scalded
½ cup melted shortening
⅓ cup sugar
1 teaspoon salt
5 to 5½ cups sifted enriched flour
2 eggs
2 tablespoons grated orange peel
¼ cup orange juice
• • •
1 recipe Orange Filling (see below)

Soften active dry yeast in *warm* water or compressed yeast in *lukewarm* water. Combine milk, shortening, sugar, and salt. Cool to lukewarm; stir in about 2 cups of the flour and beat well. Add eggs one at a time, beating well after each. Stir in softened yeast, orange peel, and juice. Add remaining flour to make a soft dough. Cover; let stand 10 minutes.

On lightly floured surface, knead dough 5 to 10 minutes or till smooth and elastic. Place in lightly greased bowl, turning once to grease surface. Cover; let rise in warm place till double (about 2 hours). Punch down. Divide dough in half; cover and let rest 10 minutes.

Roll each half in a 12x9-inch rectangle, ¼ inch thick. Spread with Orange Filling. Roll each half of dough as for jelly roll; seal edge; cut in 1-inch slices. (For pretty spirals, give bottom of each roll a poke in the center before placing in pan.)

Place cut side down in greased muffin pans. Cover and let rise in warm place till nearly double (45 to 60 minutes). Bake in hot oven (400°) about 12 minutes or till done and golden brown. Remove from pans and serve warm. Makes about 2 dozen.

Orange Filling: Combine ½ cup sugar, ½ cup chopped walnuts, 1 tablespoon grated orange peel, and ¼ cup melted butter or margarine. Spread on dough.

Tops with fruit

Toasted Coconut Bars sport jackets of Grape-Nuts and coconut, make a crunchy sweet accompaniment for a fruit bowl.

Or serve these bread "cookies" with mugs of cold milk to the after-schoolers.

To make, mix 1 cup flaked coconut and 1 cup Grape-Nuts (or chopped walnuts). Remove crusts from 4 slices day-old bread; cut in 1-inch strips.

Dip strips in ⅔ cup sweetened condensed milk till well coated and roll them in the coconut mixture.

Place strips on a greased cooky sheet. Bake in moderate oven (350°) about 10 minutes. Makes 15 bars.

Hot Garlic Bread

1 loaf French or Vienna bread
1 or 2 cloves garlic, minced
½ cup butter or margarine

Slash bread on the bias in ¾-inch slices, *but don't cut quite through* bottom crust. Cream garlic into butter; spread generously between slices. Wrap loaf in aluminum foil or slip into paper sack. Heat in hot oven (400°) 15 to 20 minutes or till piping hot.

For outdoor cooking, wrap loaf in foil and place on the grill until hot, turning bread frequently.

Garlic-butter Slices

In oven, melt ½ cup butter or margarine in an 11x7x1½-inch baking dish (if using another size, have butter generously cover bottom). Remove from oven.

Add 1 or 2 cloves garlic, minced. Arrange six 1- to 1½-inch slices of French or Vienna bread in baking dish, turning once to butter both sides. Let stand about 10 minutes; heat in hot oven (400°) 10 minutes.

If cooking outdoors, melt butter in shallow pan on grill; add minced garlic. Toast bread on grill; dip both sides into butter.

Or for *Garlic Rounds*, cut hard rolls crosswise in ½-inch slices. Fix as for Garlic-butter Slices. (See picture page 103.)

Bacon Twists

2 cups packaged biscuit mix
8 strips bacon, cooked, drained, and crumbled
1 tablespoon grated onion
½ to ⅔ cup milk
Bacon drippings

Combine biscuit mix, bacon, and onion; add milk. Mix just till dough follows fork. Turn out on surface lightly floured with biscuit mix. Knead ½ minute.

Pat or roll dough out in an 8x10-inch rectangle ¼ inch thick; cut rectangles in half lengthwise, then in ½-inch strips. Roll each strip gently with palms of hands to form pencil-like strip. Take two strips and twist together in two or three ropelike twists. Place on ungreased cooky sheet. Brush with bacon drippings. Bake in very hot oven (425°) about 10 minutes. Serve hot. Makes 20.

Crisp Caraway Logs

Using 1 package refrigerated biscuits, cut biscuits in half; roll each part into a 4-inch pencil-thin stick. Brush with milk.

Coarsely crush 1½ cups crisp rice cereal; combine with 2 teaspoons salt and 2 tablespoons caraway seed, celery seed, *or* toasted sesame seed. Roll sticks in mixture. Bake on greased cooky sheet in very hot oven (450°) about 10 minutes. Makes 20.

A good salad go-with can be as simple and easy as these!

Toasted Crackers

Select rich round crackers, crisp rye wafers, saltines, or other crackers. Brush tops with melted butter or margarine; sprinkle with one or a combination of onion or garlic powder, caraway, celery, dill, poppy, or sesame seed. Heat on a cooky sheet in moderate oven (350°) about 5 minutes.

Parmesan Toast Strips

4 slices bread, toasted
¼ cup butter or margarine, melted
½ teaspoon onion salt
• • •
1 cup corn chips, finely crushed
¼ cup grated Parmesan cheese

Trim crusts from toast; cut each slice in 5 strips. Combine butter and onion salt; roll strips in mixture. Combine crushed chips and Parmesan cheese; dip one side of strips. Bake on cooky sheet in hot oven (400°) 5 to 8 minutes or till crisp. Makes 20.

Curried Wheat Squares

¼ cup butter or margarine
½ teaspoon curry powder
Dash ginger
20 spoon-size shredded-wheat biscuits

Melt butter in large skillet; blend in curry and ginger. Add shredded wheat and toss to butter. Heat about 5 minutes over low heat, stirring constantly.

Rye Curls

With very sharp knife or slicer, cut tiny "icebox" rye loaf in *paper-thin* slices. Place in single layer on baking sheet. Dry in slow oven (300°) till crisp and edges curl. Takes about 30 minutes—check now and then.

Herbed Chips

Place large potato chips on baking sheet; sprinkle with marjoram, thyme, or basil. Heat in moderate oven (350°) 5 minutes.

Toasted Crackers—quick!

If you serve crackers hot, they'll taste twice as good with a cool salad bowl or fruit plate. Extra good with herb fix-up.

Offer crisps in handsome servers

Here little tidbits, crunchy and piping, look important—and they are! Curried Wheat Squares fill the "paddle" at left, Parmesan Toast Strips, at right.

A salad sandwich makes a meal. Or a dandy snack for afternoons or evenings when you ask folks in

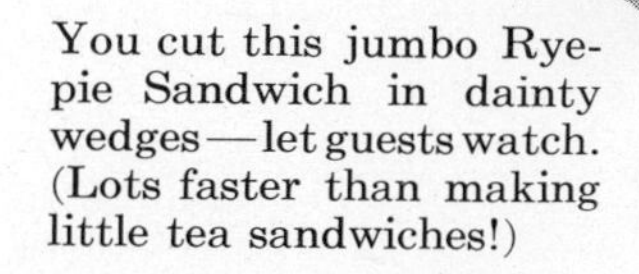

You cut this jumbo Rye-pie Sandwich in dainty wedges—let guests watch. (Lots faster than making little tea sandwiches!)

Frosted Sandwich Squares

Trim crusts from 16 slices of sandwich bread. Butter one side. Spread 4 slices, butter side up, with Egg-salad Filling. Cover each with second slice; spread with Ham Filling; cover with third slice; spread with Chicken Filling. Top with fourth slice, butter side down. Wrap sandwiches in aluminum foil; chill several hours or overnight.

Before serving, cut sandwiches in half. Stir two 8-ounce packages cream cheese to soften; blend in 6 tablespoons milk; beat smooth. Spread generously over tops and sides of squares. Garnish each with a ripe-olive flower, green-pepper stem and leaves (see picture on page 12). Makes 8 servings.

Egg-salad Filling: Combine 4 chopped hard-cooked eggs, 3 tablespoons mayonnaise, 2 teaspoons prepared mustard, 1 teaspoon grated onion, ½ teaspoon salt, and dash of pepper.

Ham Filling: Combine 1 cup ground cooked ham, 2 tablespoons minced pimiento, and 2 tablespoons mayonnaise.

Chicken Filling: Mix one 5-ounce can (½ cup) boned chicken, ¼ cup chopped celery, ¼ cup mayonnaise, 2 tablespoons pickle relish.

Lobster Fantans

Cut 4 or 5 oblong soft rolls crosswise in 4 slices *not quite to the bottom*. Spread cut sides with butter. Fill with Lobster Salad (page 104), substituting 3 tablespoons chopped green pepper for the celery, and adding 2 tablespoons minced onion and ½ cup cubed Swiss cheese. Wrap in aluminum foil and place on baking sheet. Heat in moderate oven (350°) 20 minutes or till hot.

Rye-pie Sandwich

Slice a big, round rye loaf (about 10 inches in diameter) crosswise to make a ¾-inch slice. Spread with soft butter or margarine. Mound Salmon Salad in the center. Spoon ½ *cup* of the Cheese Fix-up around salmon (see picture above). Spoon on Egg Ring, then remaining Cheese Fix-up.

Snip chives or green-onion tops over outer circle of cheese. To serve, cut in wedges. Makes 8 to 10 servings.

Salmon Salad: Mix ½ cup drained, flaked canned red salmon, ⅓ cup finely chopped celery, 2 tablespoons chopped pimiento, 1 tablespoon French dressing, dash of salt.

Cheese Fix-up: Drain 1½ cups large-curd cream-style cottage cheese. To the cheese, add 1½ to 2 teaspoons prepared horse-radish and dash salt to suit your taste.

Egg Ring: Mix 3 chopped hard-cooked eggs, 1 tablespoon mayonnaise, 2 teaspoons prepared mustard, and ¼ teaspoon salt.

Here are special-purpose salads

On chilly winter days, hot ***oven and skillet salads*** *hit the spot*

In the mood for something fancy? These salads go ***to a party***

For back-yard barbecues, ***outdoor specials*** *like these*

For the crowd—salads that ***serve a dozen*** *or double easily*

No last-minute rush if ***make-aheads*** *wait in refrigerator*

Index

J

L

M

O

P

R

S

T

V

W